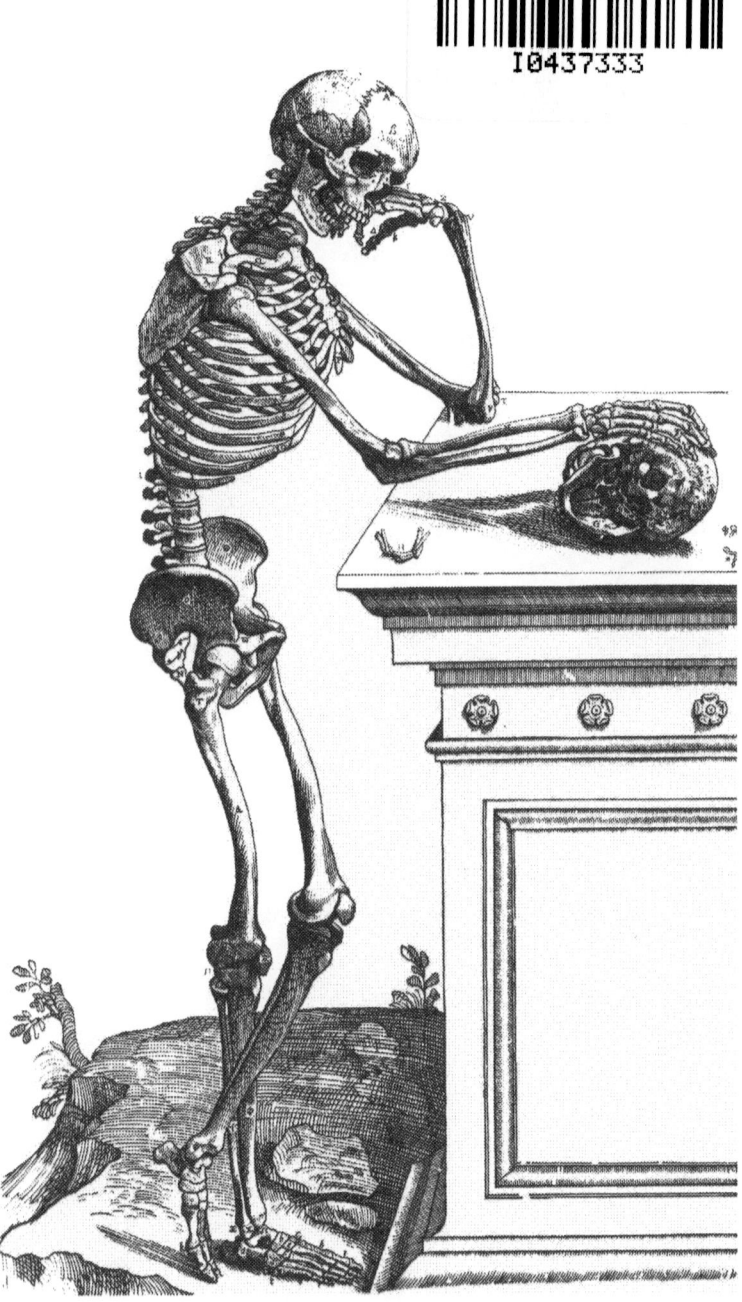

BARE BONES

The Next Step in Our Psychological Evolution

Justin Paul Chauvin

Bloomington, IN  Milton Keynes, UK

AuthorHouse™
1663 Liberty Drive, Suite 200
Bloomington, IN 47403
www.authorhouse.com
Phone: 1-800-839-8640

AuthorHouse™ UK Ltd.
500 Avebury Boulevard
Central Milton Keynes, MK9 2BE
www.authorhouse.co.uk
Phone: 08001974150

First published by AuthorHouse 8/31/2006

ISBN: 1-4259-5897-4 (sc)

*Printed in the United States of America
Bloomington, Indiana*

This book is printed on acid-free paper.

Contents

Introduction

In this series of short dialogues I use the word 'unconscious' many times. What is the meaning of this word? you might ask. The concept that is meant is usually referred to as the subconscious, which is a term I refuse to use because it seemingly gives this dimension of the mind a physical place, that is, below consciousness. Although metaphorically this may be correct I prefer the more realistic, concrete name: the unconscious mind. But still, what does this terminology refer to? I see it as anything that occurs in the mind that we are not conscious of. If we are conscious of something it is something we can knowingly identify as occurring in our mind. Conversely, if we are not conscious of something that is taking place in the mind, i.e., a thought, a thought process, an association and the like, we are unconscious of it, that is, it takes place in the unconscious reaches of the mind.

As for the validity of what is written in the pages hereafter, whether it be fiction or non-fiction, I will leave up to you, the reader, to decide.

July 2006

Which Reality

Jose sat quietly on the floor of my studio; he had his back against the wall to the left of my TV set. It was not on. I on the other hand was sitting on a chair; I was facing Jose. He was reading a book. I glanced at the title. It read: "An Introduction to Wicca." I watched him read for a few minutes before he noticed my stare. He looked up, closed the book and set it gently in his lap. Our eyes met then suddenly his eyes darted around a bit as if he were thinking. Suddenly he re-engaged eye contact and in a soft voice spoke,

"Do you believe in magic?"

It was a very blunt and direct question and after a moments thought I said,

"No. Do you?"

"Perhaps, but this book reads like nonsense to me. But really, you don't believe in any type of magic?"

I gave it some thought then answered,

"That really depends on what exactly you mean by

magic. Now if you had said sorcery I would have been inclined to answer 'Yes, I believe in sorcery.'"

I sat back in my chair. Jose looked a bit confused. After a moment he said,

"Aren't they the same thing?"

"No way. Magic doesn't exist, yet sorcery does."

"I don't understand what you mean."

I took a deep breath which gave just enough time to think up a beginning for my explanation. I said,

"My definition of magic would ideally be that magic, the very action of creating or even witnessing a so-called magical event, would have to be an occurrence that took place despite, and thoroughly breaking a given rule of reality."

Jose took a moment. He seemed to be debating in himself what question to ask next. Finally, after a long pause he asked,

"But isn't that also the definition for sorcery?"

"No," I paused and in my brief escape from the conversation I knew what to say next, "I'm not just talking your every day reality as it is perceived by most people. So-called magical acts may seem to most people as a mystery, an act that seems to them to be unexplained by the model of reality they a projecting on the world around them.

"So, in answer to your question let me continue. The acts of sorcery may seem magical by my definition of magic, but they are not. All events can be understood by at least one model of reality or another and, if they aren't, that simply means that there is no being operating with that model of reality. So, in essence, sorcery does exist and, magic by my definition does not. Got it?"

Jose did not take any time to answer,

"I think so, but if no one has a reality model to fit a given event how can that event be considered a reality?"

"What? You think reality waits around for someone to make it real?" I said jokingly to Jose. He seemed flustered so I did not wait for a reply to continue talking,

"I will tell you what I think is the case with reality. I can conceive of four types of reality, 1) being 'free reality,' 2) being 'individual reality,' 3) being 'shared reality,' and 4) being 'pseudo-shared reality.'" I stopped. Jose nodded his head which I took as a sign that he wanted me to continue. So I did,

"The first type—"

Jose cut in in a hurriedly fashion, "Wait, wait, wait! In your explanation about magic you presupposed something."

"What?"

"You took for granted that I knew what sorcery was. See, you never gave me a definition for sorcery, which I'm still confusing for magic."

"OK. I'll try to come up with a definition that will clarify my explanation for you…" a moment or two passed and I was at a loss for words so I just figured that I would blurt out the word "sorcery" and see what followed, "Sorcery is… well… sorcery is an action or event which when witnessed or experienced leads the individual to believe that a magical event has occurred, and I mean magical in the sense that I defined it, but in reality—'free reality' as I'll explain in a moment—is explainable by some true model or rule of reality. Does that make sense?"

"Yes, but I do have one question."

"Go on."

"You said 'true model' of reality. What does that mean? I mean how can there be a false model of reality?"

I took a deep breath, "Well, a true model of reality exist when an individual interprets reality as it actually exists—"

Jose interrupted, "OK I think I got it. So if an individual's interpretation or model of reality mismatches with actual reality that would be a false model of reality."

"Right, but a person's model doesn't have to match with what I call free reality for it to be a true model in their mind."

"Of course. And I think I know where you're headed with your explanation of free reality so go on and explain."

"I will but, I'm not going to begin with free reality."

"Why not?" Jose asked.

"Because if I explain individual reality first you'll

have an easier time understanding free reality, not to mention the other two types."

"Ok then, go on."

"Individual reality is the perception of an individual who interprets free reality and in the process of doing this transforms free reality into an immediately perceived custom reality, which is custom to the individual in question. This implies that in the process of this transformation, i.e., the transformation that takes place between what enters through our senses and what we perceive, the actual independent free reality does not change per se, but our individual perceptions dictated by our lifelong training in reality, and what filters we use shape and define reality into something that fits into our conceptions of reality in our own minds. Therefore the reality we see is not, in essence, a free reality."

Jose seemed pleased with my explanation when suddenly he spoke as if something had gotten his curiosity up. He said,

"You spoke of filters. What exactly did you mean? I got the rest of what you said, but I just didn't understand what you meant by filters. Did you mean we filter out input from our senses?"

"That's exactly what I meant. Do you want me to get into further detail?"

"Certainly. I must say I'm intrigued as to how something like that might operate."

I was happy to go on. I said,

"There are these operational units in the psyche

which I like to call 'mental filters.' They dictate what we do and do not see. Of course, the other senses, besides sight that is, also have these filters but, for the sake of brevity I will restrict myself to the term 'see.' And there is another mental operation which can be filtered."

"What is it?" Jose asked.

"Thought!"

Jose looked shocked. He said,

"Although I still don't know how these filters work I feel shocked by the proposition that our thoughts can be filtered."

"As you should be. That type of filter, although sometimes useful, can be quite a hamper on perception, but that's true of all the metal filters, even the ones that merely deal with the senses."

Jose said, "We seem to have gotten side tracked."

I agreed and asked if I should continue my elucidation on mental filters. Jose said yes, so I continued,

"Let's start with a nonspecific example to generalize the topic. It can be said that if an individual is confronted with a scene or situation that they cannot handle or cope with the scene will go unnoticed and the situation will not be understood to its fullest extent. Now, with that general idea out there I'm going to ask you a question. What part of the mind does this and, how does it do it? Don't answer. Just think about it." After a moments pause I said, "Well, what do you think?"

Jose said, "I haven't got a clue."

"Well, think about it. If something is filtered out

from our conscious mind, meaning: it does not enter consciousness, what part of the psyche is most likely to have control of this filtering faculty?"

Jose didn't know, so I rephrased the question,

"Consider this. If the act of filtering took place consciously we would notice it, right?"

Jose smiled, "OK, I think I've got it. Is it the unconscious?"

"Yes! That is exactly it. But, I have another question for you."

"OK, ask away."

"Does this hypothesis mean that our unconscious mind receives sensory input before our conscious mind, and the filters it through to our conscious mind?"

"I don't think you can expect me to answer that in an entirely correct manner, but it must be so."

"Perhaps, but that was only a rhetorical question to help get you thinking. Anyway, back to the subject at hand, or would you rather gravitate on that last question?"

"Well I'd like to consider it a little."

"OK, we will. Do you think it's correct to think that if the unconscious mind does receive sensory input before our conscious mind we could extrapolate that the unconscious mind lay en route between our senses and our conscious mind?"

"That seems feasible."

"It certainly does. But, that is only the easy answer, and it may not be true. Although it would explain why our conscious mind only receives a small fraction of the input from our senses at any given time; in essence why we hear one sound while another is occluded from our awareness."

"That does seem to correlate with my analysis," Jose said.

"Perhaps not, but let us delve a little deeper. If we consider directed awareness we can assume that this creates a dynamic relationship between our conscious and unconscious mind. That is they both take part in what is sensed. For example: we could search out our environment for all the sounds being made in our presence, thus making what enters our consciousness a consciously directed phenomenon. Yet, we still may find that certain sounds remain occluded from our awareness."

"That means that no matter what we do our unconscious mind is our master," Jose said.

"That may be so, but what can we do?"

"Nothing, I suppose. But what were you saying before about how our unconscious mind may not lay en route between our senses and our conscious mind?" Jose asked.

"Well, do you know what working memory is?"

"I've heard of it but I must say I really don't know what it is exactly."

"Neither do I, but I can say that it is something like short term memory. As far as I know it is like a buffer system that keeps information in our short term memory while we are working on something related to give us the ability to comprehend. For example: when you read a sentence your working memory keeps track of what you just read as you read on so that you can connect the meaning between words in the sentence. But that's just a guess, in reality I don't know, but for my explanation on filters it will suffice."

"Then I'll accept it for now."

"Good. So, to extrapolate further we could say that instead of the sensory input entering our unconscious first it may instead go directly to our working memory where it would take a place in our conscious mind, for a brief moment that is. Once in working memory the input, once evaluated by our conscious mind can either be designated as rememberable or erasable, and since our working memory acts as a buffer it can be deleted if our mind so wishes."

"You said our conscious mind determines whether or not the input is erased, that contradicts something you said earlier."

"You're absolutely right! I must amend that statement. I should have said that while I am at this given state of knowledge I can't say which part of the psyche is responsible. The different hypotheses that we've covered so far make it nearly impossible to know."

Jose said, "To this I must agree. Now let's get back to our original topic."

"Not yet," I said, "There is one more aspect of filters that I would like you to consider, but these are more like adjusters than filters. To illustrate their function I will give you a somewhat outlandish example."

"Go ahead." Jose said.

"Consider psychic premonitions. If an individual gets a premonition, how do they know it's a premonition? To the trained mind they will be interpreted as exactly what they are, a premonition. But to the untrained mind they will appear quite differently. They may, or I should say, they will most likely be interpreted—if they're noticed at all—as a psychological event that pertains to current time, that is, in reference to the moment the premonition makes itself apparent. Thus, the premonition will probably be acted upon immediately, or discarded completely as being a non-sequeter event. So, as you can see, these adjusters work to fit information into our model of reality. This, by the way, leads us back to the type of reality I presented to you first. So why not get into the second type I was going to tell you about."

Jose said, "Please, do go on."

"OK. Free reality, you could say, is the state of reality when no entity is observing it. But of course when someone does interpret free reality it does not cease to exist as a free reality. It remains as it is outside of human consciousness, while on the other hand—as we've already discussed—individual reality remains confined to the mind.

Jose smiled. He said, "I think I've got it. Free reality is the state of all things when they are not observed and analyzed by man or any other entity. And it seems this reality can only exist in two states. Firstly, it exists when no entity is judging the reality in question. Secondly, it exist when an entity is judging it, but it remains separate from the said entities judgments, which is to say that it remains free insomuch as it is itself and remains in this free state regardless of what individual reality the mind is imposing on it. And, I think I can be safe in assuming that this true reality can never be witnessed by any individual. Am I right?"

I said, "It seems you hit the mark quite well. But may I ask what makes you say that that true reality can never be witnessed?"

"Because as you said about individual realities there are all sorts of mechanisms in our psyche that filter and modify our perception of reality."

"That's quite right. May I add something though?"

"Certainly." Jose said.

"As you might come to see, individual reality may be the only type of reality available to man regardless of how many examples of reality types I can come up with."

"In that case let us move on to those two other types you mentioned so that I might come to that conclusion for myself."

I consented, "Then let's discuss shared reality. Shared reality is similar to individual reality in one respect; that is, it is not a free reality, it conforms to our preconceived conceptions. But it differs in the fact that the preconceived conceptions of more than one individual come into play and in affect are equivalent. Thus, the individuals perceiving the shared reality are in theory experiencing the same reality as reality is defined by our preconceptions."

Jose said, "Then shared reality occurs when two or more people are experiencing the same exact reality under the rules defined by the pretext of an individual reality?"

"Exactly. But, as you'll see in a moment shared reality is totally theoretical—as are all realities that we've discussed or will discuss—and most likely never occurs. I mean besides the facts of relativity as dictated by Einstein that state that two people are always experience a relative reality. Therefore, two people cannot occupy the same space and thus things will always look different for different people as they occupy different space. Besides this there are many—and I mean billions if not trillions—variable reliant structures in the brain which make a shared reality a total fantasy."

"What do you mean by variable reliant structures?" Jose asked.

"A variable reliant structure, when referred to when discussing mental processes, can mean one of two things, both of which are applicable when discussing this postulated situation. The first would be the neuronal structures of the brain, which are variable reliant in the respect that they are constantly in flux when we are concerned with the neuronal firing patterns and when, and how they are stimulated. The second would be on a lower order, that is, they are probably interrelated and dependant on the neuronal firing patterns. For our little conversation we could call them associational dependencies, which without intervention, education or certain stimuli, are constant and definitely different in every individual."

Jose said, "I understand. What you're saying is that due to these mental dependencies no two people can experience the same reality because no two people have the same exact personality makeup."

"Exactly. And this leads us to my fourth type of reality; pseudo-shared realities. Pseudo-shared realities are just what the name implies. That is, even though a reality is shared it does not need to be exactly the same for the individuals involved. The pseudo-shared reality is a realty, keeping with the rules of the individual reality, which can be agreed on between two or more individuals, and yet, even though the conceptions in each individual's mind is dissimilar in at least one way, it can be agreed upon in a basic context. This type of reality is very common and active between many individuals."

Jose said he understood and also said, "So, what you're basically saying is something like what would happen when, for example, one person asks another person a question. The person who answers the question must resort to joining the asker in their individual reality in order to comprehend the question and answer it, and this procedure results in a pseudo-shared reality."

I smiled and said, "Very true!"

I was very exited that Jose had grasped the idea so well.

Jose said, "Is there anything else?"

"I don't think so."

"OK. I'll return to my book." He did, and that was the end of our conversation.

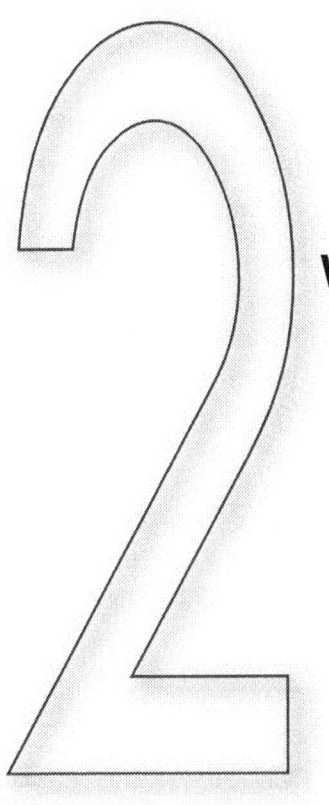

What Do You Think

Today Jose brought his friend Cote to my studio. He seemed very bright; he also had an interesting topic to discuss, although I don't know how we came upon talking about it.

He had said that years ago he had worked for a man doing manual labor, and this man was always asking, what seemed at the time, Cote said, was a rhetorical question. This question was "What do you think?" and until recently Cote never really considered it as a direct question in need of an answer. He said that he merely dismissed the question upon hearing it, although, he didn't know why. Upon reflection he stated that it might have been something in the tone of his boss's voice, or his bearing or some other thing; but he could not place exactly what it was.

Anyway, recently the question had popped into his

mind and he felt the urge to answer it. At a later date Jose confided in me that this is the true reason that Cote wanted to see me; to help him find an answer to this question.

When Cote brought it up and recounted the details of his dilemma to me I was elated. I had recently been considering the details that make up human consciousness and in my personal inquiry I had touched upon the subject of thought and how it operates. So I asked Cote,

"What do you think you think?"

He answered, "Well I think of many things."

I asked him to be more specific. He answered,

"I think about when I'm going to do my laundry, or I think about my job, and my girlfriend crosses my mind a lot."

So I said, "There you have it!"

He looked confused. I decided to relieve him,

"You're not really doing any thinking there."

"What do you mean? It sure seems like thinking."

I thought about giving him my definition for thought but decided to hold off. Instead I opted for guiding him through some of my own thought processes—if they can be called that. So I began,

"Well, to sum up what I meant by saying that, we need only look to your own description of what you think about. You said 'crosses my mind' when you mentioned your girlfriend, and I'm willing to bet that

that's all that happened, not just in that example but just about any example that you could come up with."

Jose, literally silent up till now spoke, "What do you mean?"

Cote chimed in, "I'm lost myself—I mean I get what you're saying but it just doesn't fit with my way of thinking, could you elaborate?"

"I'll try… the things that you say you think about really involve no real thought. As you said they cross your mind. But, where do they come from? you're probably asking yourself, right?" They both nodded. I continued, "They originate in your unconscious mind. All data, whether it be when to do your laundry to what your going to eat tonight to what subject your going to major in in college comes from your unconscious mind." I felt myself hashing the discourse so I paused and lit a cigarette, gave it some more thought, then continued, "Let me go back to a point in time to when you haven't got all this goop bubbling out of your unconscious. Let's say you just learned that your girlfriend is going away on vacation for a month. Then she leaves, hugs and kisses and a goodbye. Three weeks go by, then suddenly a thought crosses—note the word I just used—your mind. It is 'When do I have to pick her up from the airport?' You could assume that you thought up this question, but you did not! The input 'she will be back in four weeks at ten p.m.' has set up a time marker in your unconscious, and this marker is prioritized by the subjective importance of your girlfriend, and the subjective importance is prioritized by countless other factors, such as a feeling of love or extreme infatuation, and a fear of loss which stands by itself and is also intertwined with your feelings of love—by the way the fear of loss is instinctual—and many, many other factors; factors you couldn't even imagine. And, not only has the subjective importance of your girlfriend played in this mishmash of factors. As a further metacategory there could be your sense of duty, or loyalty… the list goes on and on. And mind you, these factors I have given you are mostly, if not totally, unconscious workings—that is they occur without you being conscious of them—but, wham bam once they become initiated by the input that tells you you should pick up your girlfriend from the airport the idea, not the thought, but the idea, comes into your mind under the volition of your unconscious mind, and your so-called conscious mind tells you to pick up your girlfriend… Does that make sense?" I knew that it did but I wanted to see if they understood.

Jose was the first to speak. He said,

"I think so, but let's hear what Cote has to say."

Cote cleared his throat. Then he said,

"So what you're saying is that anything that comes into our conscious mind is merely a product of our unconscious minds workings."

"That's exactly what I'm saying."

"Then it would seem that the individual does not think at all, but my intuition tells me that this is not so."

Jose spoke up, "It certainly seems so!"

I said, "Maybe not. Let's hear what Cote's intuition is telling him."

Cote said, "I really don't know. By all appearances you excluded thought from being a viable entity, but I think that there must be some type of thought. Can you clear this up?"

"Certainly." I said. "Just think of the chess player. He thinks, as do many others with different professions, but let's concentrate on the chess player since I think he would make the most appropriate example. We'll start from the beginning, that is, the beginning in terms of how I explained the origin of ideas. A chess player has a multitude of choices when looking at the board which he is playing on. You could call his input the layout of pieces on the board. Now, from his past experiences and learnings his unconscious mind has a bunch of possible moves available to him. Depending on his proficiency, which is also unconscious, his unconscious mind might supply his conscious mind with one move, and he will make that move. In this case there was no thought involved. But, if his unconscious mind supplies him with two or more moves he must choose. This is where thought comes in.

"Thought is merely the ability to orient what your unconscious mind supplies you with. What I mean is, if your unconscious mind supplies you with, let's say, two choices your only conscious ability, or thought process, is to concentrate on one of the two choices for a moment and wait for our unconscious mind to supply us with the intuited outcome of the choice, then concentrate on the other choice and wait again for the same procedure to take place. After this the unconscious mind will allow one of the two choices to feel more appropriate in our mind and we will choose the one that feels more appropriate. Do you understand?"

Cote answered with a question, "But how does the mind know which of the two choices is appropriate?"

"It's all unconscious," I said. "The unconscious mind takes the two possible choices and after each one is concentrated on, it reacts, in other words it, the unconscious mind, gives us the feeling that whichever it is more comfortable with is the one we should choose..." I began to see a flaw in my argument, namely that thought does exist. Which I now realized it doesn't.

Cote now spoke, "So the only thing that can be considered a conscious act of thought is the minds ability to concentrate?"

I cleared my throat, "A moment ago I thought so, but I have come to see a flaw in that thesis."

Cote went on, "So the mind is capable of other modes of thought?"

"No, that's not what I meant. Thought doesn't exist is what I'm implying."

I felt devastated. How could I have missed it—Cote broke in on my thoughts,

"But you just went through a quite detailed description on how it does exist but in a limited form."

"I know." To myself I felt quite foolish, but I didn't let it show.

"Describe your new position for us. I know I'm interested."

Jose said he was interested as well. Without having much time to gather my thoughts I concluded that I would start from the position of the chess player. I said,

"Let's consider the chess player again. If you recall, I said, 'his only thoughtful capabilities were the ability to concentrate.' Well it has occurred to me that the volition to concentrate also is derived from the unconscious. What I mean is that all action has its origins in the unconscious."

Jose spoke, "But how can that be? I act because I want to. Don't you Cote?"

"I think so, but this conversation has me doubting everything."

I spoke, "Don't go about doubting everything. Everything I have said is based on logical thought."

Cote agreed, as did Jose. I went on,

"The chess player's concentration is based on either an unconscious will to win or to lose. So when he decides on one choice over the other, he is not consciously choosing, as he might believe."

Cote said, "So, he is driven by his unconscious intent?"

"That's right. Consider this, as a child, perhaps he had some sort of inferiority complex. This, of course, did not dissipate over time. So whenever he played chess, he played to win. This was perhaps what seemed to be a conscious choice to win, but the choice was really driven by the unconscious desire to be dominant, not inferior. Now, on the other hand, let's say he was conditioned thru unconscious learnings and feelings to be a compassionate child. In this case he would perhaps be driven by the unconscious desire to let his opponent win so that his opponent would feel good about himself. So in essence either choice would be predetermined by the chess player's unconscious desires. And this fact would eliminate my previous definition of thought."

"Quite interesting," Cote said.

Jose said, "Cote, I guess you'll have to go back to your old boss, and when he asks you 'what do you think?' you'll have to say 'nothing, nothing at all!'"

We all laughed together. Jose asked Cote if he was ready to leave. Cote nodded. We said our goodbyes and Cote offered his thanks for clearing the matter up, but I refused and said I should be thanking him for helping me clear up my own views.

A few days later there was a knock at my door. I wondered who it could be; Jose always called before he stopped by. I answered the door, and to my surprise Cote was standing there. I said, "Hey Cote. Where's Jose?" I looked around; Jose was nowhere in sight.

Cote answered me, "I came alone. Jose couldn't make it."

"Well what can I do for you?"

"Well… can I come in?" He sounded a bit nervous.

In order to make him more comfortable—for we didn't know one another very well—I said in a calming tone, "Please do. Take a seat. Let me know what's on your mind."

He took a seat facing my favorite chair. I sat across from him. He said, "Something has been troubling me since a little after the last time I saw you."

I said, "Go on," in a very inquisitive tone.

This seemed to draw him out a little; he was markedly more relaxed than he was when I answered the door.

He obliged me, "Well after I gave our discussion a little thought I came to a most disturbing conclusion."

"And what would that be?"

And he flatly stated, "That there is no such thing as free will."

I smiled a bit in a losing battle to control my jovial inclinations. I said, "Now that sound's interesting. Tell me what brought you to that conclusion?"

"I was thinking about what you said about the chess player and I took that basic model of describing someone's thought processes, or lack thereof to be more specific, and started applying the model to every so-called thought process or planned action, and it seems that all possible real or imagined thought process's are invariably under the direct control of our unconscious education. I mean every thing I could think of, every single thought manifestation that I could imagine could be traced back to some unconscious influence, or dare I say unconscious control... But tell me what you think—if I may use such a seemingly inappropriate statement."

"Well, not yet. Instead, let me serve the function of helping you sharpen your own ideas. Does that sound favorable?"

"Sharpen away," Cote said.

"OK. I got what you were saying, but you seemed to concentrate too much on thought processes. Although you did mention planned actions at the beginning of what you said. I think you know what you meant as you were speaking, but take me for a fool. Consider the idea that I didn't know what you meant. Consider that from what you said about the unconscious controlling all of a person's thoughts; how could that be related to free will? You mentioned actions once and in no way did you explain how they would be affected by the unconscious. So, the fool that I am, I did not understand how free will, which would supposedly be the controller of our actions, is so invariably untenable as a viable entity. So, with this said would you please elaborate?"

Cote took a deep breath as if he were preparing himself to delve into an abyss. He said, "Let me think of a suitable example... Let's see... I'll go with my own wish to come here today and see you, and the choice I made to take that action."

I laughed, "So we'll be dealing with introspection—one of my favorite things, I must say."

After a moment Cote said, "Well my mind seems to fail me. Can we forget that last example I was about to make, for a while at least?"

"Sure."

"Instead, I have a much simpler example in mind that you will probably relate to considering our last encounter. I'll use the example of the chess player that you described for me and Jose. Now, let me see if I can break it down properly. You first pointed out that the chess player has a multitude of choices and that these choices are supplied to him by his unconscious, which has furnished these choices out of his own experiences and learning's."

"Yes. I remember. Although I don't believe I went into such detail as you just have."

Cote replied, "Despite the differences between our dissertations, do you accept what I just said as valid?"

"Definitely."

"Then I'll elaborate a little further on that point. It would seem to me that we have no conscious control over what we learn; everything from our environment enters our unconscious. So, for better or for worse, in the right place at the right time or the wrong place at the wrong time, we absorb it all. So my first point is made, that being that we cannot control what we learn."

I butted in, "Although what I'm about to say may be rhetorical I'll say it anyway just to make clear in your mind that what you think is correct is really correct. So, you say we can't control what we learn, but I say, out of foolishness, what about the book we choose to read or the TV show we choose to watch? What about those such situations?"

Cote smiled and said in a jubilant manner, "I came prepared for you. We don't choose to watch that show or read that book. That much could be extrapolated from what you said during our last encounter."

"Break it down for me, don't just extrapolate."

"OK. All learning's previous to the moment in question, that is, the moment when we pick up that book or turn on that TV, we are subject to a behavioral trend set into motion at a very young age. This trend, of course, does not remain static over the years or even over a few seconds. It is instead a dynamic entity, constantly being re-routed and adjusted by each new learning or experience; much like how the shores and bed of a river are constantly shaped by the flow of water."

I smiled and said, "That was indeed well put, and I must say you got your point across without going into some boring case history type explanation as I'm usually inclined to do."

We both laughed. Cote went on, "So this trend is what prompted us to pick up that book or turn on that TV show."

"I totally agree, and even though that was your first

point, I think that in it you explained the whole of your thesis."

Cote remained silent for a moment. Then he said, "Perhaps. But let's see if I can't be milked for something more, even if it's just a smidgen of a fact. Perhaps you can think of some way to further sharpen my ideas."

I thought it over, and then said, "You indicated that the behavioral trend is initiated at a very early age and although I know the answer to this I'll ask you anyway. What initiates the trend?"

"I don't know, but let me see if I can reach a conclusion thru some deductive reasoning. First of all, the trend must be initiated by something, and that something must be the basis of the trend itself. So it would stand to reason that experience, namely, unconscious experience—"

Here I cut Cote off, "What about conscious experience?"

"I don't see how that has anything to do with our discussion."

"I do. Take for example any skill, such as typing. When you first learn to type you do it all on the conscious level but over time as you practice you begin to do it automatically—"

And here Cote cut me off, "So, conscious learning's eventually become unconscious?"

"Yes. But further more they were always unconscious, even from the first moment your fingers touched the keypad. The practice only fortifies the skill in your unconscious so that you could perform the skill more proficiently. Even though that could in some cases be unnecessary. What I mean is that the very first time you learned the finger movements to punch the right keys your unconscious had it down pat."

Cote looked confused. He said, "Then how is it that we cannot exploit that skill immediately?"

"My theory is that the mind has a fear of losing control, however superficial that control actually may be. But that is a discussion for another time. Get back to what you were saying."

"As you wish. I was saying that the base for the behavior trend of the individual must be related to that trend. So, I take it that as our experience builds up we develop the capacity to maintain a trend."

I said, "That's exactly right. I could go into more detail, but I'm tired. So, if you have no further questions or theories I would like to get some sleep." I looked at my watch. Cote did the same. He said, "I didn't realize it was so late. I'm sorry to have put you out."

"You didn't put me out one bit. Besides, this was all quite enlightening. Oh, and later this week talk to Jose. I plan to go into detail with him some of the theories we skimmed over or ignored, ok?"

"I'd be delighted," Cote said as he made his way to the door.

We said our good-byes and I let him out. I headed for bed.

Potential

Jose had been in my studio for a couple of hours; we were watching the television. Suddenly he turned to me and said, "I'm tired of the TV. Let's talk about something."

I replied, "What would you like to talk about?" as I turned of the TV.

He sighed, "Oh… anything."

"Well. OK. Let me tell you about the capabilities that are encompassed by your unconscious mind."

"Sounds interesting enough. Go on."

"OK. Before we get into your potential let me tell you a little story that may wet your appetite to the whole matter."

"Go on."

"Once, I was involved in a rather strenuous activity

with another individual. After a while I was growing tired, but I felt I might let the other person down if I told them I wished to stop. But, eventually I grew too tired. So I said to this person that I wished to stop; but I didn't say it with my own usual self specific type of dialogue. Instead I used a term that was a ritual part of the other person's dialogue. Do you have any idea why I did that? And mind you I did not do it intentionally." I sat back and waited for an answer.

Jose said, "I really don't know."

"You should. We've been dwelling on the subject in question for quite some days now. But let me give you a clue. If something, some thought, about initiating an action, comes to your mind and you decide to follow through with it, what part of your psyche is responsible for initiating the action?"

"I would have to say the conscious part. So if the action takes place, and you did not intend for it to, it would have to be the unconscious that is responsible, right?"

"That's right. But let me make it a little more complex for you. I did consciously choose to tell him that I wanted to stop."

Jose spoke, "So it was the terminology you used to achieve your desired goal and not the act of making the statement that was not under your conscious control."

"That's right. But I tell you, with a little forethought I could have made the terminology my own, but alas, I was not thinking ahead, or was I?"

"What do you mean?" Jose asked.

"I mean that I may have been evaluating the whole situation in my unconscious many moments before I spoke. Consciously I knew I wanted to stop, but unconsciously I was evaluating most, if not all, of the factors involved."

"I understand that, but what made you take on the dialogue type of the other person?"

"Now that's the interesting part. Would you like to take a guess?"

Jose replied, "I am clear on the fact that your unconscious made your words come out as they did but I'm at a loss as to how."

I smiled, "If only more people were willing to admit they were at a loss more often the world would be a different place. I myself could use a little humbling. But anyway, back to the topic at hand. My assumption is that my desire not to let the other person down fueled the whole matter of my phrasing. It would seem that I unconsciously created my phrasing for that moment out of that desire. So, my unconscious made an assumption, or perhaps an educated guess, or even maybe out of strict trial and error empirical knowledge, that if I used the other persons terminology I would invoke sympathy by way of their own self experience; that is to say that by using their dialogue I would create an air of kinship, of sympathy through self understanding on their part."

"I understand," Jose said, "but let me see if I can or can't summarize the whole event for you. You were tired and wished to stop your physical exertion, but were worried about letting the other person down. Next, you began the maneuver of telling this other person that you wished to stop, and before the words came out—and I assume it was only a moment or two before, otherwise you might have noticed and stopped yourself, or at least modified your terminology—your unconscious mind supplied you with the words. Is that right?"

"Totally."

"The one thing I can't understand though is how your unconscious mind was smart enough to take such a complex task and manage it without trouble. I mean there had to be a great many variables."

I said, "That may be a discussion for another time. On the other hand you may figure it out for yourself after I tell you about the immensity of your potential once you begin to utilize your unconscious workings. Well, let me give you a demonstration of the capabilities of your unconscious mind, and let me tell you, they go far beyond the demonstration I am about to give you."

Jose sat back in his chair and said, "Go on."

I said, "Don't get too comfortable, I'm going to have you take part in this little experiment."

He said, "I hope it isn't too difficult."

"It shouldn't be. Tell me have you every had the occasion to speak in a foreign accent, I mean I know you strictly speak English, but have you ever perhaps done an impression?"

Jose smiled, "I've done more than that. When I

was younger I had a Spanish friend, and after being a close friend with him over the course of a few years I developed the ability to speak with a strong Spanish accent. At the time I thought it was cool and I sported this accent on many occasions."

"Good. This may be exactly what we need for our experiment, but one other thing before we go on. Can you still utilize the acquired ability to use that accent?"

Jose took a deep breath; I knew by this sign that he was thinking. He spoke, "I doubt it, but I could try."

"Please do."

He took another deep breath and blurted out a word in Spanish. I don't know what it meant for I have no tongue for foreign language, but he said it with a slight accent. I said, "That won't do. It is far too easy to use an accent when speaking in the language that the accent pertains to."

Jose grimaced; he said, "Then what should I have said. Don't expect me to use another Spanish word; that's probably the only one I know."

"What I want you to do is say a word in English using the Spanish accent. That should be far more difficult."

"What should I say?"

I said, "Oh, let me think... What would be a difficult English phrase to say in a Spanish accent? I know, say 'How are you?'"

Jose looked daunted, and with a troubled look began

to speak. He made a mess of it. I smiled and went on, "See how much trouble that was?"

He smiled, obviously half embarrassed with his display. He said, "I knew I wasn't going to be able to do it."

I replied, "Of course, that's what I was counting on!"

Jose saw me laughing and said, "Don't make fun, that was embarrassing."

"I can imagine. But in any case it has served our purposes so far."

Jose frowned, "You mean you meant for me to get embarrassed?"

"No, not at all. I mean your failed attempt."

"I don't see how that has gotten us anywhere," Jose replied.

"You wouldn't, and you won't until we reach the end of our experiment."

"Well then, let's get on with it."

I thought for a moment. Then said, "OK. I want you to prepare yourself because when I'm done instructing you I want you to act immediately. Is that ok?"

"Of course."

I went on, "What I want you to do at this moment is clear your mind and just listen. Now, get ready to say something, but try not to formulate the words until I give you the cue to. Remember I want you to use a Spanish accent. Get ready, right after I tell you what to say I want you to say it. Say 'come here.'"

Potential

Jose said it with an accent that was less effective than when he spoke a single word in Spanish. I said, "Good, but not what I truly wanted. I was hoping that we could get a perfect accent out of you; after all, when you were younger you could probably speak with a very, very accurate accent. Am I right?"

"Yes, if I remember correctly."

"OK then. Let's try a similar but somewhat different technique."

Jose sighed, "Well I am growing tired of this. After all, it does seem quite pointless."

"Patience, patience. I want you to say the very same thing that you just said, but this time initiate the action of saying it and as the words begin to come out just sit back, relax, and close your mind off from the words coming out of your mouth and just think of speaking in a Spanish accent. Go ahead."

Jose said, "How are you?" in a quite pronounced accent.

"Good, good. If you try that often you'll get even better and, as you practice the technique you can apply it to any accent you may hear."

"Wonderful. But what was the point of all this?"

"I was merely showing you a rather superficial ability of your unconscious mind; that is to say that this ability to do things that you consciously can't do is only superficial when compared to some of the more complex acts of your unconscious mind."

"I see. The act of speaking with the accent was taken

over by my unconscious when I withdrew my conscious mind from mediating the whole affair."

"You are most correct. But now, shall we get on with your potential for developing your unconscious mind to accomplish many feats?"

Jose answered, "Sure."

"I can start by citing an example or two. Have you ever had the occasion to play catch with a baseball, or football, or any type of ball?"

"Of course. I used to play catch with a baseball when I was younger, hasn't everybody?"

"Well, maybe not, but anyway your experience with playing catch will do. Now, on separate occasions I imagine you were not always the same distance from your throwing partner."

"Of course not."

"Now remember, on these separate occasions did you, each time you threw the ball, think to yourself: 'I've got to throw the ball this hard and at this angle to make the ball catchable for my throwing partner?'"

"I can be certain that I didn't."

"Good," I said, "Now what part of your psyche do you think was responsible for all those calculations?"

"I can say with confidence that it was the unconscious part of my mind."

I smiled. "And you stand confidently correct. Don't you find it amazing that from your conscious view of things all those computations, all those variables are dealt with by a seemingly automatic part of your mind?"

"Yes. It seems amazing that the mind, whether it be acting consciously, or as in your example unconsciously, can handle so much."

At that moment I thought of something. "I must tell you, it may not be handling as many variables as you think."

"What do you mean?"

"I'll tell you, but I'll have to give you a little history before we can get into that."

Jose said, "You've got my ear."

"Well that's good to hear!" I laughed at the irony of our consecutive phrases that seemed to be a play on words. I continued, "I believe that the unconscious, when compared to the conscious mind has many aspects of functionality; that is to say, it can work in different ways, perhaps either one at a time in conjunction with your conscious mind or all at once; in any case we may find out whether it is one or the other thru our dialogue. It may seem that we have two minds operating at once, either working separately or together, one at a time or both at once. With this said lets discuss the possibilities.

"If the unconscious mind is working in tandem with the conscious mind, they may seem inexorably intertwined, but let's see if we can come up with at least one example of this taking place. Do you have any ideas?"

Jose looked surprised at my asking him. He answered, "Let me think... Could it be that when we are dealing with any environmental situation our conscious mind is trying to think of ways to deal with the situation while our unconscious mind is thinking of the very same thing through conscious spurring by the conscious mind toward the end of making a judgment or a series of judgments that will supply the conscious mind with the answer or an answer made up of possible choices that no doubt, as we've already seen, will be sorted through and picked from by our unconscious mind regardless of our conscious mind's endeavors."

I smiled, "That sounds entirely feasible, but not what I was looking for. You seem to have answered a question that I haven't asked yet."

"And what question would that be?"

"Well, though your explanation seems to explain the two minds working in tandem, it truly does not. Perhaps I should have asked the question differently. In any case, you explained parallel processing between the two minds. What I wanted was an explanation of how the two minds might work in a seemingly intertwined manner; that is to say: in a way that both minds are functioning as one unit, that's what I meant by saying 'intertwined.'"

Jose replied, "I see. But I can't think of any way in which the scenario you just described might be played out in mental terms."

I said, "Let me see if I can think of something...

OK, I've got it. Let's use an example of sorts. Say you are thinking of how to answer my question, the one I just asked you, ok? Now consciously you are directing your mind—we'll use this in our example even thought, as we learned, it is impossible to direct your mind or even think—to look for an answer. Now, your conscious mind being what it is has no idea what to do—"

Jose broke in, "What do you mean by saying 'being what it is has no idea what to do?'"

He seemed almost offended at the proposition that his conscious mind might be an idiot; probably an unconsciously driven response. I replied, "To put it bluntly, your conscious mind is very incapable of running your thoughts and is rather dumb. Most, if not all of your conscious workings are just products of your unconscious mind. But come now, you know this. We covered it the other day with Cote."

Jose seemed to relent a little. He said, "Yes, I remember. But, you never said that the conscious mind had no idea what to do, you simply stated that it was supplied with everything by the unconscious."

"And so it is."

Jose sighed, "I'm afraid I must admit I'm a little lost. Would you please explain to me just what it is you mean by saying that."

"I'll be glad to. In any case that would bring us to the point that I wished to conduct this discussion under anyway. So we'll start with some history. Only the history we'll be dealing with now will take back to childhood and I had hoped to get away with telling you a limited history at most, so get ready to listen. OK?"

"Since I'm curious about it I'll be glad to listen."

I said, "Good. When you were a child, and I'm talking very young, you were without doubt exposed to language. Now, when you heard words being used do you suppose that heard them with your conscious mind? Don't answer, just listen. Whether you heard them with your conscious mind or not doesn't really matter. In either case the words were either directed from your conscious mind to your unconscious mind, or were directed to your unconscious mind directly, bypassing your conscious mind. After a given period of time your unconscious mind began to associate these words with objects in your environment."

Jose said, "What about actions?"

"Those come later. At the point in time I'm talking about the unconscious mind is not ready to handle abstractions, only direct associations. Once these associations were made you were ready to speak, and I'm sure you did. Now, in your unconscious mind these word associations began to build up. So at first you could only say one word at a time, but as the associations became more complex and began to overlap or connect with each other you developed the ability to cross connect associations and, as this happened you began to understand concepts, or better put, abstractions. This complexity of association in your unconscious mind gave that part of your mind the ability to supply your conscious mind with sentences because you could now use verbs, just as your unconscious mind supplied your conscious mind with the one word object associations earlier. Do you understand?"

Jose said that he did.

I went on, "Tell me now if you still think that your conscious mind is very smart?"

"It would seem non existent from your point of view."

"Not at all. It merely doesn't do anything, yet it is there observing passively. Even if it could do something it would not be very good at it without help from the unconscious."

Jose said, "I think that if I apply this to what you explained to Cote the other day I do understand."

"Good, good. Now let's get back to our original topic or one of its offshoots if we got sidetracked. You already covered parallel processing, so at this point let's continue with what I was saying about you answering my question and how that could be put in a light that would explain it in terms of the conscious and unconscious mind working together."

"But from what you just said I took it that the conscious mind was just an observer."

"Ah, you're quick. In that case let me put the issue in terms of how the unconscious mind might mediate such a phenomena, and we'll forget the rest. OK?"

"That would make sense."

I went on, "I've explained how the unconscious

learns to a limited degree. Let me go into more detail. The unconscious is like a sponge, it absorbs everything that is perceived by the senses. It also has its own intradevelopmental capacity; that is, it puts the information it gathers together, most likely utilizing associational properties that may or may not be innate. What I mean by that is the associational properties of the unconscious may be inborn or learned. I tend to side with the idea that they are learned. The reason I believe that is due to simple deduction. Take for example something that we've already dealt with; the learning of words. When you first hear a word it may have some value only as just anther stimulus coming in through the senses, but as we hear it over and over it becomes associated with some object that is either exterior to ourselves or perhaps a part of our body. Eventually, as we learn more and more words, and develop the ability to associate concepts or abstractions to some of these words, the unconscious mind catches on to the fact that it learns and rationalizes thru associations. Thus, we now have what I call the conscious unconscious. What I mean is that the unconscious now has the ability to reason within itself. Then by simple logic you can extrapolate on how the unconscious operates when faced with just about any problem. So, what do you think?"

"I get it," Jose said, "But I still can't imagine how that relates to the problem that we put forth; that is the problem of how my mind might be capable of answering the question you put forth."

"That's easy once you know the basics. So I'll proceed from what I've just said. The unconscious, having learned just about any idea, concept or stimuli you've ever perceived or deducted from your environment—internal and external—has the ability to rationalize any answer to any question or problem it encounters, and that implies psychological drives as well. So your unconscious can and does posses the ability for you to answer, given the fact that you have acquired the knowledge necessary thru experience and also the fact that it's given a proper road or thought outlet to facilitate the expression of your ideas, or as in this case the answer to a question."

Jose asked, "What do you mean by saying a proper thought outlet?"

"Well, suppose you have an unconscious idea, but lack the words to put it in. The idea would remain stagnant as far as waiting goes, but by saying stagnant I don't mean it is not subject to change; it can change. Maybe a variable here or a variable there or perhaps even a full re-evaluation. But anyway, without the proper means to express the idea it cannot come out of that stagnant state. That is not to say that it cannot become conscious in some cases although if it did you still would not be able to express it; it would remain just a fuzzy abstraction in the mind. But, if you learned a proper dialogue formula that would allow for the expression of the idea the idea would then become expressible."

"I understand."

"Back to it then. So in regards to the subject at hand you can see how the unconscious mind would supply you with the answer. But let's use a simple model to capitalize my point. Take a simple question, like: what did you eat for breakfast? Now, that question seems easy enough to answer, doesn't it?"

Jose said, "Certainly."

"Ah ha, but it's not. When you ate your breakfast your unconscious recorded the whole event, as it does at all times. Now, when asked the question you may seem to be searching your memory with your conscious mind, but this is just a pale reflection of what the unconscious is doing, and I dare say that without the unconscious mind we would just sit here staring into space like an aphasic. But anyway, the unconscious reconstructs the event of eating breakfast, and having heard exactly what the question was supplies you with the answer and makes you say it, or not say it; that all depends on the temperament of your unconscious. So, in regards to you answering my question, you must not have either the proper experience or the proper outlet, or perhaps you lacked both; I say this because you could not answer my question despite your willingness to."

Jose said, "I get it."

"Good. Now let's return to the beginning of our conversation; I think you're now prepared enough, or should I say experienced enough to understand what can be accomplished once you begin to utilize your unconscious workings. For example, you can choose what you wish for your unconscious to supply you with. Listen to this idea: say you want to respond in a certain way to a certain stimulus. Now, when you're in the situation in which you wish to act in that certain way you must remember to choose to act as you wish and respond in the way you want. Do this a few times and the very act of acting in the way you want will be absorbed by and engrained in your unconscious. Then you will notice that once you are in that situation you may be supplied with a choice to act out that action, the choice being furnished by your unconscious mind, or you will automatically act in that way under the guidance of your unconscious. Of course you can't count on being able to do something like this consciously all the time, I mean besides the fact that the conscious mind is just a passive observer, if it weren't it would be incapable of supplying you with the choice of making the proper response all the time. For that you must wholly rely on your unconscious, which is if you taught it properly, or should I say if it taught itself properly.

"Speaking of teaching your unconscious, imagine the possible behaviors or thought patterns that could be programmed into it. You could make yourself into almost anybody you want."

Jose's interest seemed to pique at this idea. He asked, "And how would one go about doing that?"

I answered, "You should be able to extrapolate that for yourself from the example I just gave you. But, in any case I'll give you another example. Then we'll leave the remainder of this conversation for some other day. I'm going to give you an example that's quite similar, actually a simulacrum of the last example I gave you, only I will go into exactitudes. But I may need some help. Tell me, do you have any behaviors you would wish to adopt into your personality?"

Jose retracted in thought. He was silent for more than a few moments. Then he spoke, "I would like to think of eating less often; as you can see I've been gaining weight."

"That's not what I'm looking for. Although, I could answer you. It would merely take a readjustment of your association chains in your mind, but that is for another discussion. For now, limit your wants to a physical behavior."

"Well," Jose said, "this is somewhat similar to what I just said but I think it will work out; it is after all a physical behavior. I would like to remember to drink a tall glass of water before my meals, so in effect I will eat less."

"That I can work with. All you have to do is in the beginning of your change, tie a string around your finger, any color you wish as long as it gets your attention. Now, in your mind associate the string with your desired behavior. After you do that; and do it thoroughly, you should, every time you see the string, be reminded of what you want to do. Of course, there are more effective ways of doing this, namely, association chain readjustment. That technique is far better and less likely to malfunction, but I'll explain it to you another day. The current technique I am showing you is laborious and can in certain instances malfunction. Given the nature of the psyche you might accidentally associate the string with eating instead of drinking a tall glass of water, and thus begin eating more as you get reminded of eating by that silly string on you finger. Otherwise, if this technique works, you should get reminded of drinking water before you eat, and after a given period of time you can remove the string and the association that was created by the string's presence, namely that you drink before eating, should remain intact as long as you left the string on long enough to condition yourself to elicit this response as an unconscious occurrence, that is to say that your unconscious has learned through experience to supply your conscious mind with the alternative of drinking before you eat. For the rest, let's leave that for another time; I'm tired of talking. What do you say we watch some more TV?"

Jose nodded, turned toward the TV and after pressing a button it came to life.

Association Chains

Jose had just arrived at my studio and, as if he couldn't wait, he immediately said, "I want you to tell me about the association chains you mentioned the other day."

Not having remembered that I mentioned that particular notion to him I asked, "What are you talking about?"

He said, "Remember? You mentioned them to me when we were talking about the potential of my unconscious mind."

I remembered. "Oh, yeah. So, you want to discuss that, do you?"

"Certainly. I'm quite interested in learning about them."

I began, "OK then. But first let me tell you about

thought tracks, which would be a precursor to me telling you about association chains."

"OK, go on."

"Well, a thought track is much like a sound track. It is there, in your mind, playing in response to self stimulation, external stimulation or a combination of the two. It works in a similar way to the functioning of the unconscious supplying the conscious with material, just as it was in the case we discussed together with Cote. Do you remember what I am talking about?"

"How could I forget?" Jose said.

"Good. Now, your main thought track, that is, the one you are aware of, resides in your conscious mind during some periods of time, and during others it resides in your unconscious."

"What determines where it is located?" Jose asked.

I replied, "It all depends on what you are doing. Take for example you just sitting there. Now, do you suppose that you are aware of what you are thinking?"

He took a moment, then answered, "Sometimes."

"Exactly. And think about this; when are you aware of what you are thinking?"

"When I concentrate on my thoughts..." Jose momentarily grew silent, and then continued, "... or, sometimes when I'm just relaxing and letting my mind wander."

"And would you say that during these times you are conscious about what is passing through your mind, or to keep true to our topic I should say: what thought track is playing in your mind?"

"Definitely."

"And when would you say that you are unconscious of your thought track, that is, when do you not notice it?"

Jose replied, "When I'm doing something physical, like working."

"OK. Would you then agree with the statement that at these times your thought track is unconsciously playing?"

"How would I know?"

I said, "I can offer you proof. When working, do thoughts ever just randomly enter your conscious mind?"

"Of course."

"Well, where do you think these thoughts come from? They are fragments of your thought track that have in a seemingly random way entered into conscious view. Why they have done this you will see in a moment. To continue let me say that in your mind there are multitudinous smaller variables that sit in the background of the psyche. The thought track that you can be aware of is the culmination of these smaller intricacies that has been built up like a pyramid. These smaller more numerous variables, which are constantly shifting, add up to smaller and smaller numbers as you go up the pyramid. The variables as they add up coalesce into larger fragments, which could be labeled concepts or abstractions, and as they add up we reach the top of the pyramid which is the total fluent culmination of our thoughts, i.e., the thought track. Now, can you answer me if I ask: why do these thought intrusions occur?"

Jose took a moment. He said, "Logic would indicate that these intrusions are merely the culmination or final product of the build up of smaller thought fragments."

"Yes, but you did not answer my question. What makes them intrude on a nearly silent conscious mind?"

"If I had to answer, I'd say that the thought track had been built up of enough smaller parts to make its appearance unavoidable, or to put it another way, there was enough behind the though to make it roughly break through whatever else was occupying the mind."

I smiled. "That's my theory as well. Now let us get back to my elucidation of thought tracks. What do you say?"

"Tell me exactly what these parts are that build up to culminate into a thought track."

"As my theory would have it, the smaller parts are associations. Of course they become more and more simple as you descend down the pyramid; and conversely, they grow more and more complex as you go up the pyramid and thus, you have this setup to thank for the series of factual stops your mind comes to when you are in repose."

Jose said, "OK, I get it. But one more thing. You said that the thought track plays in response to stimulation and, you enumerated three types of stimulation. Could you describe them for me?"

"Sure. The first I mentioned would be self stimulation. This type of stimuli comes from within the mind, that is, the current thought track is reacting to itself."

"But how can something react to itself?" Jose asked.

I said, "Simply. Think about this: when you begin to speak a sentence and have not yet formulated the words to complete that sentence, what does your mind do to come up with a fully fluent sentence? It reacts to what words came before the current moment and creates the rest of the sentence thru association; this we could call a speech track. And so it is with thought tracks as well."

Jose said, "So, in this case the though track thru association continues on in a fluent manner, constantly generating itself from what came the moment before."

"That's true, but you will find that it is only true for this specific case. As for the other types of stimulus we will consider external stimuli next. External stimuli can be any thing in your environment, that is, anything in your environment that influences your thought track. As theory would have it, everything in your perceivable environment does in fact influence your thought track whether you are conscious of it or not. Remember when we discussed how the unconscious is aware of everything that your senses perceive?"

"Yes I do."

I continued, "Well that theorem stands up in this

case as well; as I should have said when I was describing internal stimuli, that is, everything in your unconscious always contributes something to your thought track, and that is true for all three examples I will give you of stimuli types. But in the case of external stimuli the unconscious is stimulated by external activity in contrast to internal stimuli which causes the smaller unconscious parts of the thought track to react to themselves as I have dictated. Do you understand so far?"

"I think I do. But what could be classified as external stimulus? And I want you to go into detail; don't just say that an external stimulus is what your senses perceive. I mean, I understand you, but I want to be clear on the subject."

"OK, let me think… say your thought track is currently running an association chain—which I'll explain later—that lets you think about something… help me out; give me an example of something that you might think about Jose."

"OK. I might think about what I'm going to eat later."

I said, "It will have to do. Firstly, what makes you decide what you are going to eat later? Your thought track! Spurred on by your unconscious drives—just like we discussed with Cote—your thought track is given choices that you might be in the mood for—all decided for you by your unconscious of course—say Italian food comes up as the choice you're going to go with. Now, you're on your way to the restaurant, looking forward to eating some pasta; when suddenly, you smell Chinese food. The external stimulus has entered your mind, and just as suddenly as you smelt the Chinese food your thought track is telling you to eat the Chinese food instead. Now, the dynamics involved such as, the reason Chinese food trumped Italian food which might be urgency of hunger or some other factor or series of factors, or variables, whichever word you feel is more appropriate, are not immediately important. But anyway, did that example clarify things for you at all?"

Jose said, "I think so, you can go on as you wish now."

"Thank you." I said. Then I continued, "The third type of stimulus I mentioned was a combination of both internal and external stimulus. Now get ready to listen; I'm going to get into some pretty heavy dynamics here. It's required for a full understanding of how this type of dynamic relationship between stimulius and mind is created and upheld. Do you feel experienced enough in this topic to continue?"

"I think so." Jose said.

"Well, as you might not expect, thought tracks are scarcely made up of words, although that does not disclude them, for certainly the conscious product of any given thought track is commonly a word based idea."

Jose asked quickly, "What do you mean? I understood from the beginning of our conversation that the thought track is what makes up our thoughts, so, as you can see, I'm a bit confused when you say that there is a conscious product of a thought track."

"And you are right in being confused; I should have made things clearer. Tell me if the following will do. The thought track is an entity that runs in the background of the mind; it is responsible for all our thoughts, but that does not mean it is all our thoughts. It is behind everything we think and do, yet it rarely makes it into our consciousness except when we are—as you mentioned—in a state of repose or when relaxing or when we are totally distracted from our thoughts and a thought breaks through. Does that suit you?"

"Yes, definitely." Jose replied.

"To further display my preceding ideas let me continue. The thought track consist of abstract factual instances which follow one after the other from an intertwining of associationally related ideas or thought stops. But anyway, let's get back to the dynamics. I think I'll start with the product and work my way down to the smaller associations. Let's say that you have as a product thought the question of whether you're going to rent a comedy movie or a horror movie. The next lower level would be the thought track behind this question. I can't be specific because I don't know the pattern of your thought track. But I can cite an example to illustrate my point. You could have the surface thought track like this: I want to see a movie, but I can't decide which type. Now, the next lower level might be 'I'm bored' working dynamically with another thought track stimulator that implies 'I haven't seen a good movie lately.' Now, to break things down further 'I'm bored' might be broken up into smaller parts, such as: 'I haven't done much all day,' and 'I should do something.' And 'I haven't seen a good movie lately,' might be broken down into smaller parts also. Such could be something like 'I like movies,' and 'the last movie I saw really sucked.' Now, you've probably noticed that I'm using words. Unfortunately it's the only way I know of to get my point across. But, in these regions of the psyche—that is, where these thought chunks operate—words rarely flourish. Instead, your mind composes these thoughts out of blank factual stops. The word 'blank' indicating a lack of words, and 'factual stops' means conclusions. All that occurs in between these stops are thought transformations. That is, the unconscious is adding up and subtracting associations according to what makes sense and that ultimately leads to these factual stops, or conclusions, whichever words you choose to use. But anyway can you see what I mean when I say that there are a lot of dynamics involved—I mean the layers that I described for you are just the tip of the iceberg. In the lower levels there is much infighting. All of the lower order associations are competing to become either thought track material or thought track material supports which are the layers I dictated for you. Did you notice that I seemingly didn't use any external stimuli in my dissertation?"

Association Chains

Jose took a deep breath as if he weren't expecting to talk any time soon. But eventually he said, "Yes I think I did."

"The truth of the matter is that all stimulus, even of the external type, becomes internal stimulus. If you noticed I said something like: 'I haven't seen any good movies lately,' when I was pointing out thought supporters. Not seeing any good movies—like some of the other examples I gave you—is a mixture of internal and external stimulus. The phenomenon of seeing a movie is an external stimuli. Now, the movie, being external stimuli, entered the psyche and interacted in a dynamic way with your subjective experience of what you saw, and in this way became an internal stimuli as it was depicted by me. Do you understand?"

"Totally!"

I said, "Good. Now lets get on to association chains, and don't worry we'll get into some more dynamic interactions as we proceed. Are you ready?"

"Ready and waiting."

"OK. I'll get started by explaining associational matrices, more specifically, what they are made up of. To do this I'm going to have to establish different categories of associated items. Category number one would be the senses, that is, the ocular, the auditory, the tactile, the olfactory and the gustatory senses. Category number two would be the emotions, such as, love, hate, happiness, sadness, apathy, indifference and the like. Emotional memories are not just emotion though."

Jose said, "I was going to say: How could emotions stand on there own? Aren't they connected to the senses?"

"Yes. I was getting to that. Emotions are rarely remembered by themselves, they usually are dynamically connected to the subjective experience that enlivens what our senses perceive."

"So, is subjective experience part of another category?"

"No. The items that make up our associational matrices are just the basic building blocks of association. Subjective experience itself is a higher order function, that is, it is the outcome of our associational matrices workings. It could also be called the product of our associations."

"It sounds like your talking about thought tracks." Jose said.

"You will find that is true of most of what I'll say about association chains."

"Why is that?"

"Because thought tracks can be divided into associational chains, that is, the thought track is basically made up of associations. But come now, we mustn't talk in circles."

"Continue then, you answered my question."

"OK. Category three, the final category, is questionable in its standing, but I'll mention it anyway. It is instantaneously learned memories and associations."

"Could you define that for me?"

"Sure. Instantaneous learning denotes any instance where we find ourselves through, for example, shock or surprise, programmed with an instantaneous association that persist over a given period of time and has the ability to manifest itself in any situation where the prearranged stimuli are present in their original form, or a form that is similar to their original form. Is that an understandable definition?"

"You couldn't have made it clearer," said Jose.

"Good. But before we move on there is one point I wish to get across. That is, emotional charge. Emotional charge can be described as any emotion from category two that is attached, by way of association, to any memory that is stored by means of any item of category one. In other words it is any association between categories one and two that constitute a memory and means of recall, whether that recall be intentional or haphazardly associational. So far we have two definite categories, one questionable category and a point of interest. Are you keeping up?"

"This is a little complicated, but I'm doing my best. So far, I think I've got it."

"Then to continue let's contemplate the structure of an associational matrix. We'll use the idea of seeing a bird as our given example. Now, the first stage, or core, of the associational matrix is the core thought occurrence when we see a bird, and that core identification of a visual stimulus would be exclusively the mental picture of a bird. The secondary stage, or core, would contain all of the immediate associations with the visual picture of the bird; these being, perhaps, wings, feathers, yellow— the color of our given bird—and/or flight. Now, the dynamics dictating our subjective experience of seeing the bird may not allow the association between bird and flight unless the bird is actually in flight. Further more, these associations usually occur on a non-verbal level, just as seeing the bird may not bring any words to mind. The third stage, and perhaps the last, is all other associations that could be related to the picture of the bird, and, this last stage, through extraneous self introspection, may in fact lead to all other associations available in the mind."

Jose asked, "How is it possible that seeing a bird can lead to any of the available associations that reside in the mind?"

"Easy. Every single association in the mind is either directly or, as is the more usual case, indirectly connected to every single other item in the mind that is accessible thru association. I said that the indirect associations are more common because much of the material in the mind is unrelated. Such as, when you think of a car you can't spontaneously associate it with dirt, but thru exploratory association you will find that some path, however extraneous, will lead you from car to dirt. Do you understand?"

"Yes I do."

"Good. To move on then. What I have just explained about the associational matrix in our given example can be further examined. Certainly the outline of associations I gave you are not manually directed, instead they occur automatically. These associations are automatically and unconsciously associated with the core thought. Although, the individual may through conscious effort mentally travel from one association to another.

"So it can be said that when we perceive a given stimulus an associational process is initiated. And, given that no other stimulus occurs this associational process can follow any given path to any given point, but, it must be stated that the associations do not follow a random path, they continue of their own momentum, that is, just like thought tracks, the series of associations at any given point directs all future associations given the lack of outside influence. In other words, the past associations are in of themselves their own stimuli directing the next association. And that is where the usefulness of controlling what your association chains do comes in handy. But first, let's consider triggers; and maybe I'll give you a revision of what I said about associational matrices. Are you keeping up?"

"I think so." Jose said.

I continued, "I'll start with a little revision that will make the understanding of triggers much easier. If we see a bird, we see as a whole object represented in our mind by an abstract means. We do not consciously associate it with any of the secondary core items unless another stimulus is enacted in our mind, either externally or internally, which leads us to think of one of the secondary core associations, and also, such a stimulus is needed for our ideas to reach out into the complete associational matrix system in our mind. Although, one may already have in place, in their mind, an associational trigger so that when they see a bird this trigger may, for example, be the stimulus needed to carry our ideational process to the secondary core or all associations.

"Now I'll cite an example of what might constitute such a trigger. Say you have an individual who studies the flight of birds for a living, or even an individual who unofficially just loves to watch birds fly. Now, when either one of these individuals sees a bird, a trigger is set off, namely the immediate association between birds and flight is triggered. Are you still with me, because triggers are important to utilizing your association chains?"

"I think I'm still with you." Jose said.

"OK. Now keep in mind what I just said about triggers because they are instrumental in the utilization of association chains. Let's get to the crux of the matter, and that is association chains themselves.

"The term 'association chains' is almost a metaphor; in essence the term describes a mental function or thought process that could be visualized as a chain, that is, a series of items put together in sequence to form one single item or 'chain.' The links of the chain represent ideas, and the actual place where the links are interconnected—and remember: we're thinking metaphorically—is a mental transformation or thought transformation. A thought transformation is a change from one mental or ideational state in the mind to another; thus the links or factual stops are connected by these transformations, or interconnectedness of the individual links with each other. Chains can be constructed—and are quite usually haphazardly constructed—to contain these mental representations, ideas, or factual stops and mental transformations; and the function of the chain would be to take you from one idea or mental representation to another distinct—and in the case of purposeful manipulation a controllably—variable idea that can be quite remote—in the sense of distance of relativity—from the starting point idea. In fact, the ending point idea, or factual stop may have nothing to do with the starting point idea, although this is rare; the usual chains are very short and the starting point is directly related to the ending point, but in some cases and in many cases where chains are purposefully constructed, the chains can be very long and, as described as a possibility above, the ending point may not be directly or seemingly not even indirectly connected. Are you keeping up?"

Jose said, "I think my brain is overloading, but I think I got what you were saying. You can go on."

I did, "I think at this point it is only proper to give you a little taste of how association chains can be utilized, if only to keep your interest up. Imagine a chain made up of seven segments, which, of course, would be made up of six interlinks holding the segments together. The segments are factual stops, or ideational representations and the interlinks are associations, or more properly mental transformations. Now segments two through six are put in a distinct order to facilitate a thought path that will bring the individual from segment one, or the starting point idea thru all intermediate associations to seven, or the ending point idea. When this process is learned it can become streamlined through a little practice, and instead of going through the associations one by one, the chain will form a single association—at least it will be experienced as such—made up of the many smaller associations. So, it can be said that the individual has, as an operational mental function, an association that links one idea with another even if the ideas can not through traditional, or natural association, be linked together." I sat back to relax and smoke a cigarette.

Jose took this as a cue to talk. He said, "So what you're saying is that any idea can be associated with any other idea, even if they are entirely unrelated."

"And so much more," I exhaled a large cloud of smoke. "But more of that later. For now let me clarify something that I don't think I emphasized in my dissertation. Yes you can associate two extremely remote ideas but, and here's the kicker, you must find a path in between the two ideas. Of course, you would want to find the most efficient, that is, the most direct route in between the two ideas."

Association Chains

"How would you do that?" Jose asked.

"Well… introspection! And some very careful thought. In other words, you need to search your own mind association by association—and you might want to take notes—until you find the most direct path; and then you can put together your custom association chain. Once you do that you will have to run the whole route thru your mind until it becomes streamlined and automatic."

"So, what's all that seemingly hard work good for?" Jose asked.

"The obvious answer is speed thinking, but there is another function that this method can be used for, that is, skip overs."

"What's a skip over?"

"A skip over is where an isolated—and it must be isolated well enough for the item to be restrained from moving along a contingent association chain—memory or idea is placed somewhere in the middle of the association chain so that the idea can not be directly accessed, and if the association chain is triggered the idea will occur as a part of the whole chain and not as a single, identifiable thought. But there might be instances where skip overs are not always necessary. The associational path that holds the unwanted idea can be redirected to go around the unwanted item, although, this method is not as easy and effective as skip overs are. While a redirected associational path can work, the unwanted item still exist in its own right and

65

can be recalled through other contingent associational pathways, but when the unwanted item is in the middle of a chain it can not be recounted unless the chain itself is dissolved. So, what I just said is the gist of what I know about skip overs. Does it answer your question?"

"Yes, definitely. I totally understand you. Go on."

"Then let me get back to triggers, because, as I said, they are instrumental in the utilization of association chains. As I have already stated, a trigger may be needed to set off an associational process, and thus, a trigger may be needed—and probably is needed—to set off an associational chain. And even once the chain is started triggers may be needed for the associational process to move from one link in the chain to the next. That is, triggers may need to be installed in each place that one link is interlinked with another to trigger the next chain, or factual stop. In fact, this may be the very means needed to build an association chain. But once the chain is in place and triggered several times it may become streamlined leading to our ultimate outcome of having all part associations of the chain made into one single item, and then when utilized, or triggered, the chain will be experienced as a single association. Do you get what I'm saying?"

Jose answered, "I think so. What you are saying is that once a chain is constructed it can, once triggered, lead you from one idea to another—no matter how unrelated—in one single association, or to use your own terminology: one single mental transformation."

"How right. But did you grasp how an association chain is constructed?" I asked.

"I think so, but the technique was rather dispersed throughout all the other stuff you were saying."

"OK then," I said. "Let me explicitly explain the construction of a chain by way of an example. First, identify a starting point, that is, a beginning idea. Now, the starting point may need to be something natural— for the sake of ease. What I mean by 'natural' is an idea that already naturally occurs in your mind. Of course, you could train yourself to have newly installed ideas, but that is just adding more work to an already difficult process, unless, of course, you feel that you want a new idea as the starting point idea. To clarify, let me say that the first item needs a trigger. Now, if it is something that you naturally think of you probably already have a trigger for it. So we'll skip the step of installing a trigger for the starting point idea.

"Second, identify or create the second trigger, that is, the trigger that connects the first idea with the second idea. Now, it may need to be somewhat associated with the starting point, and it definitely needs to be associated with the second link, or idea. But, the second link of the chain need not be associated at all with the starting point idea, it only needs to be associated, or connected by way of the trigger.

"Third, identify the second link of the chain—and

you'll want to do this in tandem with the second step, and obviously with the fourth step; it goes like this for all steps, they must be somehow connected in order for them to lead from one to the other. After that you just go on from idea to trigger to idea to trigger to idea to trigger to idea until you reach your desired ending point idea.

"Now for a tangible example. Imagine a two link chain. The first link is the mental representation of a finch, and the second link is the mental representation of the color brown. How would you go about linking the first idea with the second? In this case we are lucky because the second link just so happens to be associated with the first link, but in any case we shall see how two links are connected. The reason I said we are lucky is because 'brown' happens to be the color of finches. So we have an easy transformation, or trigger between the two ideas. Do you know what this trigger is?"

Jose shrugged his shoulders. I went on, "It's easy. The trigger is 'What color?'"

Jose said, "OK, that was too easy!"

"It isn't always that easy. But in any case, you can see that after some practice you could install that trigger and upon the occasion when you see a finch you will think of the color brown."

"Makes sense." Jose said.

"I hope so," I said. "Would you like an example of how I applied this technique personally?"

"Why not? But, make it quick, my attention is waning."

"OK, I will. My desired ending point was introspective thought, and my selected starting point was a natural choice, it was any visual stimuli that I naturally found boring. As you will see, in this case the first link also served as a trigger trigger. So anyway, I asked myself: What transformations were needed to bring my mind from the starting point to the ending point using an association chain to facilitate the transformation? I came up with the following. Starting point was visual stimuli, first trigger was realization of boredom, second link was being in a state of boredom, second trigger was to look to a new visual area, third link was another state of boredom, third trigger was to remember my original state of boredom, and the fourth link was my ending point of resorting to introspection. Now this might be a tough one, but do you realize how the ending point was arrived at?"

Jose replied, "No. It seems like it just came out of the blue."

"It does when you only look at the surface of the association chain. It was what was happening underneath that caused me to resort to introspection. If you'll recall, there were two times that I looked at my visual stimuli, of course I couldn't help looking, it was right in front of me and there was nothing happening to trigger introspection, so there it was, the boring visual stimuli. But anyway, the second time I saw boring visual stimuli I was forced by the trigger of renewed boredom to think back to the last time I was bored which was the last visual stimuli I saw, and since this old stimuli no longer occupied my visual range in order to remember it I had to activate introspection. And so you see the whole chain culminated into my desired outcome which was introspection."

"But wasn't your introspection limited to the mental representation of a boring visual sight?" Jose asked.

"That's a very good question. To answer I'll have to say yes, but once I am in my mind—and this is a personal phenomenon that I don't automatically attribute to anyone else—I tend to free associate, that is, I seem to mentally wander off. But, as you said—which would probably be the case for most individuals—the introspection would probably be limited to that memory. In that case I would suggest adding a trigger and another link in the chain that would take the situation of limited introspection and add too it some other aspect that would begin a meaningful introspective journey."

"Very interesting, but now I'm hoping that you're finished because I am mentally exhausted."

I said, "OK, you can relax... I'm finished."

Jose sat back and sighed.

Dying All the Time

Jose walked into my studio around three p.m... We exchanged greetings, after which he took a chair facing my usual seat. I sat down.

"What's up Jose?"

"Well, I was watching a show today and the most incongruous thing happened to me."

I was interested. I asked,

"And what could that be?"

"It was a show that two or three years ago I watched all the time, but since then I haven't seen it once until today."

I said, "What so incongruous about that? Unless you mean the incongruence was that you built the pattern of not watching it over the past two years and today you've broken that congruency by watching it."

Jose laughed. He said,

"Don't jest. I'm trying to tell you about my experience."

"OK, go on."

"Well, when I watched the show today it wasn't the same type of experience as I remember having when watching the show two years ago."

This thoroughly intrigued me so I asked,

"What was the difference between the show you watched today and the show you watched two years ago?" I was leading him on.

"The show was… well… different."

"Go on."

"As I remember the show, it was quite interesting and welcoming to my attention, but today it was totally different. It seemed to have lost something. As far as I could tell it was totally uninteresting and it seemed cold, like there was no life to it."

I was elated at the proposition of dissecting this phenomenon. So I began,

"First let me correct you, then I'll tell you what had happened if you can't deduce that for your self once you're corrected."

"OK."

"The show did not change as you suggested. It is exactly the same today as it was two years ago."

"Then tell me. What happened?"

I smiled, "You changed!"

Jose looked utterly confused. He said,

"What do you mean 'I changed'?"

"It's not a simple enough matter to begin with how you've changed. So, let me begin by telling you how we are all dying all the time."

Jose smiled. He said,

"I know, I know. We, as each day passes are inevitably moving closer and closer to our deaths. Therefore, we are always dying." He seemed proud at his attempt to hit the mark I had placed in front of him. But he was wrong in one sense.

"Although you are technically correct in your summarization, you are thinking in a context that does not immediately correlate with your experience." At this point I lit cigarette. Jose, with a touch of sarcasm, said,

"OK, I'm open. Tell me how 'we are dying all the time'."

I exhaled a large cloud of smoke, put my cigarette in the ashtray and watched the smoke rise from it while I gathered my faculties. I said,

"Tell me Jose, what separates us from the animals?"

"Animals can't think, while we can." He answered quickly.

"What do you mean by 'think'?"

He paused, "I don't really know."

"May I suggest that you mean we posses the ability to rationalize, while animals are restricted to instinct?"

"Yeah, I guess that's what I mean."

"Don't be so quick," I added. "Let's define instinct and rationalism, or at least try to come to a common agreement as to what they might signify. OK?"

"OK. I'll start by trying to tell you what I think instinct is."

"Sounds good. Now let's get started." I took one final drag off of my cigarette and stomped it out in my ashtray.

"Instinct is probably what brains less developed than ours rely on to make judgments—"

I butted in, "But wait! Were you in agreement with me when I said animals were restricted to instinct while humans can rationalize?"

"Yes of course." Jose conceded.

"Then you are erring when you say that animals are reliant on instinct to make judgments."

"Why?"

"Would you say that it requires rationality to be in any position to make judgments?"

Jose sat back in his chair. "Yes! You're right. But that would meanthat animals can't make judgments, right?"

"Exactly! And that bring us to the nature of instinct." In all the excitement I had the urge to light another cigarette but decided against it. "Instinct, though its source lay unknown to me at the moment—"

Jose butted in this time, "I think it's source is in what are called the lower brain functions."

"Do go on. I'm always open to new knowledge."

"Well, as I understand it different species have differently developed brains—and what I mean by saying 'differently developed brains' is that one animal compared to any other has a brain that is more or less evolutionarily mature--humans beings are supposed to have the most highly developed brains of all animals. And I must add that you were wrong in saying we are separate from the animals."

I was delighted. I said,

"Quite right, quite right. We are just another sort of animal. But am I right in sensing that you are not quite finished with your explanation? Go on."

"Well the other animals—beside humans of course—having less developed brains are more reliant on their instinct, or lower, which would be less developed, brain functions."

"Interesting. Interesting indeed. But now tell me why you think I was wrong when I separated us from the animals?"

"You mean you don't know. I thought you agreed with—"

I interrupted, "I did. And I know why, but I want you to tell me why you think I was wrong."

"Because we too, not only the animals, can act using instinct alone in the absence of rationality. Is that what you thought?"

"Yes! We act on instinct all the time, but those actions should not be confused with unconscious behavior because even unconscious behavior is fueled by reason."

"So, after all this, tell me what you think instinct is."

I laughed, and then said, "I may not be able to tell you what instinct is, but I may be able to tell you how it operates. In any event I'll do my best."

"Go on." Jose said.

"The brain receives a stimulus through the senses and then the organism reacts without any thought being present. That is if you don't include automatic brain operations as a rational thought."

"OK, what about reason?"

"Reason—which we both have reason to doubt as a conscious phenomenon due to our little conversation with Cote—may be the ability to think matters over, that is compare options when dealing with any thought or action that requires attention as dictated by our unconscious conclusions. But we know this is all hogwash anyway. Do you remember the conclusions we came to with Cote?"

"Yes, of course." Jose replied.

'Good. Can we, in your opinion, move on to what I was going to explain to you?"

'You mean how we're dying all the time?"

"Yes," I replied. "Think about your underlying thought track. Do you think it is running in an unchangeable loop?"

"I would hope not. That might get a little boring after a while." Jose said.

"Of course it would. Now don't get me wrong, there are segments that do repeat. Although they are usually very short segments of your thought track, and mind you, once played they can never repeat in exactly the same way."

"Why not?"

"Because of myriad factors, or variables if you wish. Every impression made upon you, whether it be a conscious impression or an unconscious impression, has a changing effect on the way you act and think... forever!"

"What do you mean by forever?" Jose asked.

"Well, simply that once affected there is nothing you can do to reverse the resulting changes made in your psyche."

"That seems a little foreboding." Jose said.

"It should. Because unlike a dirtied towel your mind can never be washed clean."

"God! You're scaring the crap out of me."

I said, "Good! Maybe from now on you'll learn to censor what you allow into your mind."

"Let's just get back to the topic of dying, could we?" Jose said.

"As you wish. Just think about the last time you learned a new word that you now use as a standard word in your vocabulary. Think about it and give me an example. OK?"

"Well… I know what you mean, but on the spot I can not think of any specific example."

"That doesn't matter; we can move on anyway, but we'll have to do without a tangible example and rely on theory. The first time you learned a given word did you think of it as an impression on your mind?"

"No, I don't think so." Jose said.

"Well, it was. And once in your mind it took root—
"

Jose broke in, "What do you mean by saying it 'took root?'"

"Simply that the word's neural representation began to form associations with other concepts and ideas that are in your mind, and the connections must be made with related items. For example, let's say you learned the word 'total.' Now, once in your mind this word—although it is not immediately identified as a word in your mind, instead, the word serves as a symbol that represents the concept of the word 'total'—would naturally associate with such things as 'complete,' and, 'finished.' These, of course, are immediate associations, that is, they are directly related to the concept of 'total.' But there are other associations to be made; these being dynamic associations, that is, they are not directly related to the concept of 'total.' Now, if you add two and two you know that the answer is four and as an immediate association you would know that four is the total, but what I'm talking about here is the ability to know that if you add two and two you will get a total;

that is an indirect association because you don't yet have a total to compare the idea of 'total' to."

Jose said, "That's interesting, but what does it have to do with your concept of dying?"

"You'll see. But first let me indicate a more subtle form of mental change. Say your outside and you glance at the sun, you won't do that again without sunglasses, or take the smell of a garbage disposal dump, once smelt you will try to avoid that area, especially in the summer."

"I get what you're saying, but I still don't see the relation."

"OK. I'll get to it then. Every impression has some changing affect on your thought processes, and in certain cases the resultant actions stimulated by these changed thought processes. Therefore you are never the same person from moment to moment, and thus you are dying moment to moment in the sense that if you consider yourself your thoughts incarnate, and conversely you are being reborn from moment to moment."

"I disagree," Jose proclaimed. "I don't consider myself to by my thoughts."

"But aren't you? What do you consider yourself to be then?"

"I think I am a body and hopefully I have a soul somewhere in here."

"That certainly is a rather limited view."

"Limited though it may be, I consider it the truth." Jose said.

"But what about all that we've covered in our discussions."

"I can't seem to apply that to myself."

I said, "Well consider this. I know what kind of music you like and I'll apply that to you. In essence I'll show you how and why you like that music and perhaps in the process you see how subtle influences can have a great affect on how you think and how you can behave. Also, hopefully, you'll see that you were once one way and now because of a series of influences, or stimulus you're another way, and maybe you'll agree that your old self is dead and a new self has been born, and although the example I'll be using is not subtle at all maybe you'll accept my word that all moment to moment experience changes you. OK?"

"If you think you can do it go ahead" Jose said.

"We'll start with your childhood and work forward thru the years of your life in leaps. I'm guessing from what I know about you that as a child you held a mainly indifferent composure when it came to listening to music, that is, it didn't affect you emotionally in any way. Am I right?"

"That depends on how early you're talking, I mean was I five, six, seven, what?"

"Suffice it to say that the period I am talking about was before you entered school, and possibly the first few years of school."

"Then you're right," Jose said. "But, I don't think

any child that young has yet developed a preference for any type of music."

"I'm not saying that you lacked a preference; what I am saying is that you were indifferent, that is, you weren't attracted to music at all."

"That may be right." Jose said.

"Good. Now let us move on to when you were in school and you started noticing what types of music the other children were listening to. At this point you were still indifferent, but you began purposefully exposing yourself to the same type of music that was most popular among your classmates. Am I right?"

"Possibly." Jose said.

"Now I want you to think back. What do you think drove you to this action?"

"I really don't know." Jose answered.

"Then let me offer you an answer, although you're likely to deny it at first."

"Let's find out."

I continued, "Simply, peer pressure. The drive behind exposing yourself to that type of music is the fact that, as we learned from our earliest social experiences, we should do what all the other kids are doing. Do you deny it?"

"Not yet," Jose answered.

"And this continued peer pressure drove you to accustom yourself to that type of music. Now, you may not have even liked the music, but, in order to fit in you listened to it anyway and thus grew more fully accustomed to it. Do you deny anything I've said so far?"

Jose sighed, "I'm afraid not, but as you know from my current taste in music that pattern did not last."

"We'll see." I said. "Let's move on to… let me guess. High school! That is the most likely time period where what I'm about to accuse you of took place; any later and the music preference wouldn't have been able to take root in your mind, and any earlier and you wouldn't have had the proper frame of mind to catch on. But anyway, something happened. I don't know what, although it was probably an accident. Maybe you were just tuning thru the stations, or even better, maybe you were on a Sunday drive with your father and he was playing some older music. Now at first you thought the music was corny, just out of peer pressurized habit, but, as you continued to listen you noticed that the music wasn't so bad. In fact, you feel that it touches you emotionally. Did something like this happen?"

Jose answered, "Maybe. I can't pin it down, but I think something like that did happen."

"OK, but before I continue let me enter a side note into the record. The reason you gravitated to emotional music is not as plain as you might think; the reason isn't that it emotionally touched you, it is something else, but I will get to that later. For now let's stick to exploring your musical taste timeline. Now, remembering the way the song made you feel compelled you to search for more music that would emotionally touch you. You find the music you're looking for, and over the course of the next few years you start building up a collection of emotionally touching music from many different genres. Up till now, the present moment within which you find yourself in the here and now doubting everything I've just said to you. Am I right?"

"You've got the history right, but I'd like to hear what your little side note has to say before I commit myself to anything."

"Of course Jose. Let me explain. Why did you gravitate towards emotionally touching music? There are probably many possible answers, but here we will deal with only one—and I think it's the one that applies to you. You as a child watched a lot of TV, and from what you saw was that emotionally in-touch people are praised by others. Now whether this is true in real life or not is unimportant, you witnessed it anyway and that is all it takes. Now, through the experiences you had at school you probably learned that people who are praised are popular and well liked, and with the standards that you learned from the society a young person experiences you found this appealing. So, as the connection was made in your mind you began to search out ways of becoming emotionally 'in-touch,' and it just so happened that you discovered emotional music and because of that connection in your mind you immediately took a liking to it. What do you say?"

Jose sat back, took a deep breath and said, "Now I

think I understand what you meant by saying that we're dying all the time." He sounded sad.

"Can you be more precise? Did I kill any part of you by what I just said?"

"I feel that a part of me died while you were dictating that explanation to me. I don't think I'll ever see music the same again," he sighed again, "but certainly this feeling I'm having isn't what you meant by dying all the time, because certainly I don't always fell this way."

"No, it's not. Usually people don't even notice, but this is an acute case. I seem to have taken a large part of your personality and dismantled it to your own detriment."

"Let's not talk anymore. I want to think."

I said OK and lit a cigarette, we both sat back in our chairs.

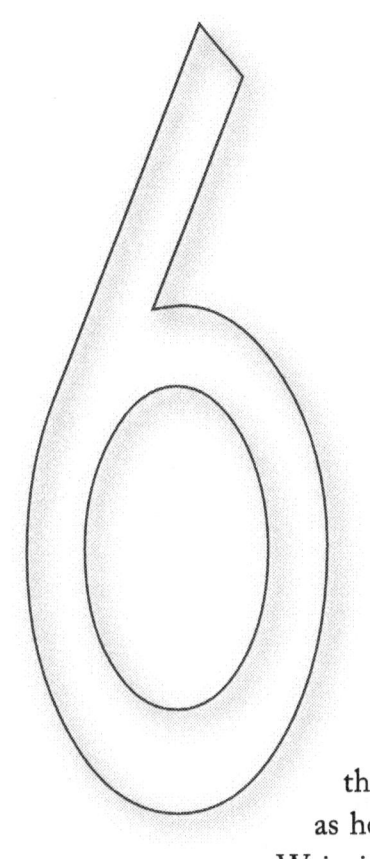

Anal Dreams

I had been waiting for Jose for some time now. I was outside my studio, sitting on the steps which led up to my door. Finally he arrived.

I stood up, descended the final two steps and smiled as he approached. I said, "Jose! Wait right there, I'll be right over."

I approached him.

As I got within a few feet of him he said, "Hey! What are you doing outside?"

I said, "We're not going in."

"Why not?"

"I'm going to show you something today, and we need to make use of a public place if it's going to work."

"If what's going to work?" Jose asked.

I smiled. "You'll see. But anyway, let's get moving."

I led the way. We walked mostly in silence. Finally we reached the city park. It was a weekend and a beautiful day so the park was rather busy. Perfect for what I had planned.

Jose said, "Are we at our final destination?"

"Sort of. I'm looking for somebody."

"Who? Is it anybody I know?"

I replied, "No," and left it at that. I could tell that Jose was getting restless, but I had something in mind and it would not work unless I found the right type of person.

We wandered through the park aimlessly. Finally I spotted a rather large rough looking individual in the distance.

"Come on," I said to Jose and led the way.

I knew that Jose was deathly afraid of violent confrontation, and that suited my purposes perfectly. We approached the man and at about a distance of ten feet I stopped. Jose stopped with me. I said, "Wait here for a moment."

I purposefully closed the distance between me and the stranger. When I was close enough I tapped him on the shoulder. He turned toward me and I proceeded to tell him that my companion had made some derogatory comments about him. His reaction was what I had hoped for. He grew angry and demanded that I point out my companion immediately. I did. I pointed to Jose who looked thoroughly confused; he did not hear what I had said to the man. The man approached Jose and proceeded to push him. The man was furious.

I broke into the conflict and said to the man, "Let me say something to my friend before you beat him up."

He agreed. I whispered in Jose's ear, "Pay close attention to how your anus feels no matter what happens." Then I backed off and let the confrontation continue.

Jose had managed to talk his way out of it after some fear driven pleading with the man. They separated. Jose turned to me and said, "What the hell did you do that for?"

I grabbed him by the arm and said, "Let's get out of here before he changes his mind and beats you up anyway despite all your pleading."

We made our way to my studio, but before we entered Jose stopped just outside my door. He said, "You're lucky I followed you this far. I'm liable to leave right now if you don't give me a good reason as to why you set me up in a situation that, as you know, I would find eternally disagreeable."

He was furious—at least as furious as his non-violent personality would allow him become.

I sat on my stoop and patted the step with my hand. "If you really must know 'why?' before you enter you should sit down. It will take a bit of explaining; and hopefully you'll see that I merely intended to teach you something. Besides, if the situation became too dangerous I would have merely interceded and told the man that I was mistaken."

I patted the step again. This time Jose sat down; he seemed to be calming down. He said, "If the lesson proves to be valuable I may just find it in my heart to forgive you." He smiled and patted me on the back. "Besides, I consider you a good friend. Now tell me what this lesson was all about."

"Well, I wanted to teach about a not too common phenomenon—well, at least not too noticed. I call it my theory of 'anal receptivity.' Did you do what I said? Did you pay attention to your anus?"

"I tried. It was difficult; I was much too nervous." Jose answered.

"Yes, but did you feel anything?" I said.

"I'm not sure; I certainly felt my heart pumping... Now that I think about it, at one point in the latter part of the experience I felt as if something was poking me in the butt. Is that what you wanted me to notice?"

"Yes! And I'm glad you did; now I can explain my theory."

Jose said to go on. I did, "When you, or any individual, gives up their own certainty in favor of another individual's opinion, especially if you know that they are wrong, you give yourself over to anal reception. That is, you basically bend yourself over a barrel for them, and this leaves you open to anal reception. And that is the feeling that you felt."

"Does it apply to any situation? I mean, what if you relent your own opinion out of love for a mate?"

"It doesn't really work that way. You have to do it against your will in the face of the consequences you would face if you didn't relent. If you do it by choice, that is, if you want to relent, whatever the situation, you will not be giving yourself over to anal reception."

"But in my situation I did want to relent; I didn't want to face the consequences so I relented out of choice."

"But you didn't really. Let me explain and you'll see why you experienced that phenomenon. You knew that you didn't make any comments about that man, therefore when he confronted you and insisted that you did you at first disagreed with him, thus setting up your certainty about the situation. And once you realized that the man would not hear what you had to say you changed your bearings and began to agree with him, which was followed with many apologies from you. But tell me, when did you start to feel the sensation in your anus? Was it at the point when you initiated your agreeing policy with the man?"

"Yes, I think it was."

"You see! You knew you were right, but you gave up on backing your certainty and, against your will, you conceded to his point of view."

Jose sighed, "OK, I get your theory, but what was it that I felt?"

"I have two competing theories—although neither may be true—as to what it was that you felt. The first—and most likely the least probable—is that another aspect of the individual is involved, that is, the second body, dream body, or as I like to call it, the ethereal wave body."

"I have an idea of what you're talking about; sort of like the soul right?"

"Yeah."

"I am familiar with the first two terms, and somewhat familiar with the third, that is, I know what you mean by saying ethereal body, but why did you use the word 'wave' to describe it?"

"Because of something called the 'window effect;' it applies to waves. It is an occurrence that takes place when two waves occupy the same space; or rather it occurs while two waves are in the process of joining. When two waves are joining, at the very last moment, the two waves vibrate differently. Before they are joined they are stable, but, at that very last moment of the joining the two waves vibrate violently in a very unstable manner. Imagine the ethereal body and what it would feel like if this body, as a wave, was in the process of trying to occupy the same space as another ethereal 'wave' body that had a different wave frequency, and mind you, the greater the difference between the waves, the more violently erratic the vibrations. These violent vibrations might be very painful."

"How do you know that this 'window effect' actually occurs when it comes to the soul? Jose asked.

"Because I've experienced it. But enough of that, let's get back to the subject we were discussing."

"That would be good; I understand your first competing theory that seems to state that anal sex is occurring between two of your 'ethereal wave bodies."

"Good, I'm glad you grasped it. But anyway, let me tell you about my second competing theory. It has to do with the symbolic logic of the unconscious mind. The unconscious mind does interpret symbols in what could be termed a contradiction, that is, it may interpret symbols in an abstract logical way, although there is no conscious thought of the symbols application. For example, if we consciously decide to uphold one belief and discount its antagonist we may, in our environment, be exposed to a stimulus that that will be interpreted as a symbol that will fortify this mental proclamation. Of course, the interpretation of the symbol and its usage by the unconscious takes place on the unconscious level, even if we notice the stimulus. And of course, it will not appear as a symbol to our conscious mind and usually go disregarded. Meanwhile, the unconscious mind is making full use of the symbol's possible applications. Regarding what I just said I will give you a relative example. The proclamation of a belief may be fortified by a fortifying symbol. Such a symbol might be a sound, such as something that would be heard on a construction sight. This sound might be the drilling together of two pieces of wood or some other material, or the sound could be a hammering together of the same. Now, as we make our mental proclamation we might hear just such a sound, which is, of course, a symbol of the completed construction of something, i.e., our proclamation. This symbol, when added to our proclamation by way of the unconscious, has the effect of fortifying our said proclamation in our psyche, thus making a reversal of our proclamation far less likely. Does that give you at least some idea of how the unconscious works with symbolic logic?"

"Certainly, but I don't see the connection to our main topic."

"Well, it's really not that difficult. You see, the feeling that you felt in your anus might be a metaphor, or symbol of what is taking place when anal reception occurs on a psychological level."

Jose said, "Ah… I see. The feeling was produced by my unconscious as a symbol for what was happening to me on a psychological level."

"Exactly," I said. "But whether it is merely a non-intellectual product of the unconscious or an intellectual attempt by the unconscious to communicate to your conscious mind what is actually happening I really don't know. But, if the theory ever proves true, I would side with the latter, knowing what unconscious mind is capable of."

"Well, I think I'll forgive you, seeing that it was a lesson worth learning."

"Then let's head inside."

We both stood up and entered my studio.

7

Prearranged Universe

There was a knock at my door. It was Jose. I said, "Hey Jose, it's been a long time."

It had been at least two weeks since I've see him. He replied, "Yeah. I've had myself buried in a book lately."

"Was it a good book?"

"It was definitely interesting. Would you like me to tell you about it?"

I said that I would, so we both took seats; facing each other of course. Jose began, "It was a book about parallel universes. I got interested in the subject after our last talk, when you mentioned the possibility of a parallel universe. Apparently it's not a new idea. According to this book quantum mechanics has predicted the possibilities of parallel universes. They seem to postulate the idea that there are an infinite number of parallel universes, each one being spawned as anybody makes a choice."

"What do you mean?" I wasn't getting what he was trying to say. "Can you go into more detail about how they are spawned?"

"Sure, sure. I was getting carried away with myself. When in any situation we have choices. We can do this or do that, say this or that, and with every possible variation a new parallel universe splits off for the choice or choices we didn't make. So for every variation of every situation there is a home in a parallel universe where that variation exist. For example, if you are at a fork in the road and you choose to go right there is a parallel universe where you went left."

I was doubtful of this hypothesis, but it was interesting indeed. I said, "I disagree!"

Jose replied, "Nobody said you had to agree. But why do you disagree?"

"I believe there can be and is only one universe. I can even back that statement with some theory of my own."

"Well, go on."

I did, "I have a theory that I call the theory of the prearranged universe. It's a rather new theory. I came up with it after Cote and I had a conversation about how free will doesn't exist. Did he tell at all about that conversation?"

"Yes he did."

"I based it not only on that, but also on the preceding conversation that took place between the three of us. You remember that conversation, don't you?"

Jose said, "Sure. The one about how people don't think, or rather, are unable to think."

"Yes, that one. But anyway, let me get on with my theory. You see from the just mentioned conversations it can be concluded that since there is no such thing as free will there can only be one predetermined universe. I know that's not much to go on. Do you want more detail?"

"Definitely. I can't make heads or tails of your theory from what you just said."

I said, "Well... You'll have to have some patience as I explain; you see I haven't written this theory down in a coherent format yet, so if it comes out in a hashed up manner you must excuse me."

"I'll do my best to make sense out of what you say even if it lacks the lucidity of a coherent thesis." Jose said with a smile.

I smiled back.

"OK. Let me see if I can explain it... I think I'll use our current encounter as the main example. As I hope you'll see from my theory we could not have changed the destined outcome that is this encounter between us. We could not have been speaking in any other manner than the one we are speaking in now. We could not be using different words. In fact you could not have avoided coming here at the exact time you did, or brought up any other topic of conversation than the one we are discussing now."

Jose quickly said, "But how is that possible? Aren't such things under our control?"

I said, "What control, Jose?"

He replied, "I could have chosen not to come here today, or to not bring up this topic. Am I wrong?"

"Deadly wrong. You see, today's events were predetermined at the very first millisecond of this universe's existence."

"That sounds ridiculous. How could such a thing be?"

I replied, a bit sarcastically, "Do you want me to just give you an explanation that's relevant only to recent events, or do you want me to start from the beginning of time?"

Jose returned my sarcasm, "Well since you mentioned it start from the big bang, or whatever it was that began our universe."

"OK." I said. "Since the 'Big Bang' is the accepted theory I guess I can start with that. OK, the big bang occurred and from that singularity that existed up until the bang, atoms, particles, electromagnetic waves, and all matter as we know it spewed forth. Now these items all projected outward on predetermined paths, that is to say in an analogy, when you fire a gun, the bullet does not go off on a random path, it moves in the direction the gun was pointed and the bullet, as it moves, conforms to resistance in the air and gravity. And so it was in a similar way that these aforementioned items moved off from that singularity in a predetermined manner."

Jose broke in, "But then doesn't that predetermined manner deteriorate with time and become chaotic?"

"No. Granted things do get more complex as you go along, but there is always an underlying order. The seemingly chaotic interactions are not chaotic at all, they follow rules. To put it simply I could say that as any given particle, for example, moves or stays still it is being acted on by all nearby particles, and in turn these nearby particles are being acted on by the particle in question and all other particles that are nearby, even the ones that are further than the one in question. So you see, all particles in the universe are interacting with all the other particles in the universe no matter how distant they are from one another, and that is the underlying order. It's not chaotic, but instead, predetermined by the starting point. Do you get my point?"

"I think so."

"Good then let's move on. Now, the atoms that spewed forth, all moving in a predetermined manner, went out into space, and in certain areas they formed gaseous clouds or stars, and in other areas they coalesced into planets and asteroids and meteors. All taking place in a predetermined manner."

Jose said, "But I still don't get how a planet or a star being formed could have been predetermined."

"Just think about how the particles and atoms I first

mentioned moved off in a predetermined manner. Did you agree with me on that?"

"Yes."

"Well just follow the path they would have taken from that very early point in the universe's life. As those atoms moved off they would all be acting on each other in a predetermined way, and thru this action and reaction the atoms would be inclined, or it would be better to say 'destined,' to coalesce in certain patterns. Do you agree with that?"

"From your theory's standpoint I would have to agree with you. But I must say that from the beginning it sounds like what you are saying is invariable fact."

"Don't be so quick to give my theory such a definite label. It is only theory because nobody knows for sure how the universe began; but I will say that for more recent events that we'll get into later I tend to view this theory as fact." I said.

Jose replied, "I think I know where you're headed with this as far as recent events are concerned. Are you going to say that we are like the atoms moving in certain directions and interacting on one another to produce a predictable outcome?"

"Sort of. But come now; since you seem to have an understanding for the basics do you mind if we discuss recent events? It's always more interesting for me when dealing with humans than when dealing with inanimate objects."

"For me as well. You can move on to more recent

events; I believe you were going to discuss our current encounter."

"Indeed, indeed. But where should I start? I know, I'll ask some exploratory questions that might lead us both into some insight."

"Ask away." Jose said.

"Well... What drove you to come here today?"

Jose took a moment to think, and then said, "It could have been a couple of things. I had just finished that book I was telling you about; as I said, that's what's been keeping me busy for the past two weeks—"

I broke in, "Stop! We'll start with that. What drove you to read that book?"

"Our last conversation. I said before that you mentioned parallel universes to me, but I think that I came up with that idea myself. We were talking about ethereal bodies and, if I remember correctly, I thought that perhaps our soul or, as you called it, our ethereal wave body might exist in a very close but parallel universe and I was off; I bought a book on the subject and dove into it."

"Good. But what drove you to think of parallel universes?" I asked.

Jose took a moment to think. "I remember! I saw a show on the television that briefly discussed the topic."

"And again; what drove you to watch that show?"

Jose answered, "There was probably nothing else on."

"OK, but, could there be some other reason? The reason I'm asking is because I know you are into science, especially theoretical science."

"Yes, I think your right. It was a combination of my interest in the subject and a lack of anything more interesting on the TV that drove me to watch that show."

"Good," I said. "Now why do think you are interested in theoretical science?"

"I really don't know." Jose said.

"May I venture a guess, for I do know you quiet well?"

"Go ahead."

"Am I right in guessing that you've always been at least slightly interested in theoretical science?"

"I think so." Jose answered.

"And that only in your mid twenties you became obsessed with it?"

"Right on, but how did you know?"

I answered, "Because I know you well enough to make such observations and calculations about your personality. But my vision has limits, for I don't know what originally got you into that topic to begin with. Perhaps you put the ability to think well on a pedestal, and thus aspire to reach such heights in your own quest for knowledge and the ability to think. By the way, that tendency was unavoidable, for something in your childhood, some event or series of events, inspired you to acquire that trait, or perhaps it was inborn. In either case I think I can begin to explain to you how we unavoidably ended up here today discussing this topic in the exact manner that we are."

"Explain away." Jose said.

"OK. Do you agree with me when I made those statements about how you acquired the taste for science?"

"Well I have no proof to the contrary."

"That will have to do." I said. "I'm about the same age as you so I can describe our childhoods in unison. When I was young I had no interest in school, and that lasted all the way through high school; and, as you know I dropped out of college. But, as I grew older I began to feel a deficit in myself. So I filled this intellectual deficit by teaching myself various disciplines. Then we met, which did not end my hunger for knowledge. That brings me close to the point we are at now. But now, it's your turn. Tell me about your quest for knowledge considering what I revealed to you about yourself. Start with your childhood."

Jose began, "Well, like you I never really was into school; I never even tried college out, I just passed it right by. But, as you described so well, I always was interested in theoretical science. This led me, like you, to search out the knowledge I was interested in—that's probably why we get along so well; because, as I know, neither of us has very many friends. But anyway, that's the basis of my life up until we met, which, like you, has not hampered my thirst for knowledge."

I said, "And we met! How fortunate for the both of us. But, our meeting was not accidental. Do you remember the circumstances?"

"Of course. We were casually introduced to one another by a mutual friend and you, on that occasion, invited me to stop by your house some time. By the way, why did you do that? I know you aren't exactly the social type."

"Well..." I had to think. "I guess its because as we were talking—on that occasion when we met—I noticed that you were quiet intelligent, and I just figured that maybe we would get into some interesting conversations."

Jose added, "Your hunch was right; we do have some very interesting conversations."

"That we do," I said. "And these conversations that we have are a great way for us to hone our thoughts."

"I must agree; I'm definitely more intelligent because of them."

"OK. What do you say; shall we get back to the subject at hand?"

"Definitely!" Jose exclaimed.

"Where were we?" I asked.

"Our childhoods."

"Oh yeah, and how we met, right?" I didn't wait for an answer. "Anyway, we couldn't have not met; as I said—to create a cliché—it was predestined at the very first moment of our universe. That mutual friend was just doing what he couldn't help doing."

Jose said, "You're speaking in trivialities, let's get to the crux of your theory so I can understand what you mean when you say: 'It was predestined.'"

"OK. We came to the conclusion that you were predisposed to theoretical science, but since I don't know what fueled the start of that predisposition we must start from just after you gained that trait. So you came over two weeks ago and we got onto that whole thing about dreams—"

Jose broke in, "I thought you were teaching me about your theory of anal reception."

"Well it was really a lesson in dreams, but that's all I'll say; I'll let you make the proper connection on your own. Anyway, you saw that show, which you couldn't have not watched—"

"Why not?" Jose broke in

"Let's figure out 'why not.' You said that there was nothing else on the TV which implies that you were bored. Now why were you bored?"

"There was nothing to do." Jose put it very simply.

""Well now, that was unavoidable. Let's look at some possible variables concerning why that was unavoidable. 1) there was nothing for you to do in your home, no toys, no musical instruments, and no good books to read; am I on track?"

"Yes, although I don't play with toys, nor do I make use of any musical instruments."

"I know; I just wanted to show you what some of the factors causing your boredom were. But to continue,

2) the television was, because of 1, the only way for you to displace your boredom. And 3) there was nothing of interest on the television, which led you to the inevitable—and I hope by now that you see that it was inevitable—choice of watching the show that you did choose to watch, and it was the only show you would watch. Do you see the inevitability?"

"Of course I do, by now it's obvious." Jose replied.

I said, "So, inevitably you watched that show and thus, the idea of parallel universes was implanted in your mind. Now, the next item leading up to our current situation was the last conversation that we had. Within which you took your impression of parallel universes and applied it to what was being said. This occurrence left you with the desire—because of your thirst for the theoretical, and your previous exposure to the topic—to explore the possibilities of parallel universes. And so, you went out and bought a book on the subject, and in your own style, i.e., your thirst, you dove into it and didn't emerge until you were finished. This took you the requisite two weeks, during which I hadn't heard from you once. But you did finish the book; and almost immediately, you were here wanting to tell me about it. Now why were you so eager to tell me about it? No, don't answer. I have all the information I need. Reason 1), you were proud of your newly learned knowledge, and 2), you wanted to keep with our tradition of having intellectual talks, which you though the information in the book would allow—it did by the way; we are here now having a quite interesting exploratory dialogue."

Jose added, "We are, but not on what I intended it to be on. But anyway, I can see how this situation was unavoidable, but, you also said we couldn't be using any other style of speech than we are now; in fact, you said it was predestined that we would be using these exact words. I still don't see how that's possible."

I said, "Well think about it; take the steps that I outlined to give you an idea of how this situation was unavoidable and apply them to your education; both in school and in life, but be more exact, that is, apply the steps only to your verbal education."

Jose thought for more than a moment, and then nodded his head.

I said, "Do you get it?"

"I think so," he replied.

"Outline it for me."

"I'll try… Let's see, I, as a child, learned words in a certain way; as did you. I learned them both in school and in life. These learning's culminated into my present pattern of speech which, as you said, and as I now see, was unavoidable. Am I right?"

"Yes! Although there is much more to it. Your teachers learned their speech patterns and styles of teaching in the same exact way, and their teachers learned their speech patterns in the same exact way, and so on, all the way back to the beginning of speech. Also, the people in your life who left an impression on your speech style learned in the same exact way from the people in their lives back thru time. So, as I hope you see the way we are speaking was predetermined."

Jose smiled, "I get it. And that theory, or model applies to all behaviors and circumstances, so that all things are predetermined."

"Exactly!"

We both smiled. I added, "Let's get some lunch, I'm famished."

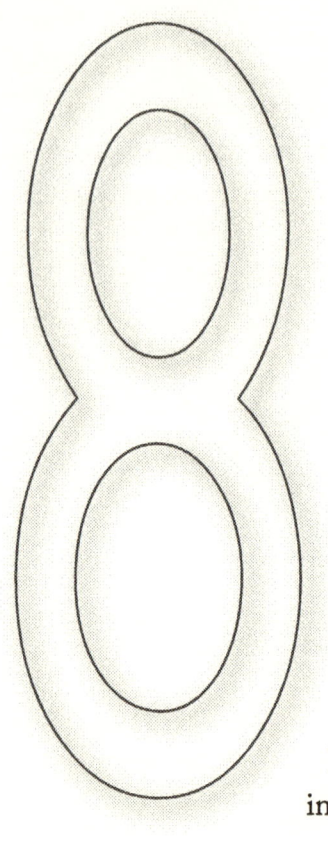

And They Knew They Were Naked

Jose asked me if I had ever read the bible. I said that I have read certain parts. He asked me if I found it interesting.

I said, "Sure... It was very stimulating."

"What do you mean by saying that you were stimulated?" He asked.

"Well, some of the topics stimulated my mind into devising some very interesting theories that could be applied to the scripture."

"Tell me about some of your theories." He said.

I answered, "I'll tell you about one; my favorite one. Have you read the story of Adam and Eve?"

"Of course."

"Good. But before we get into Adam and Eve I'll have to give you some indirectly related data."

"Go on," Jose said.

"OK, the main theory you need to know is the idea of unconscious conversations. In many cases when people are intentionally communicating between each other and in some cases unintentionally, they are exchanging more information than they know, that is, they are communicating unconsciously. Let me give you a tangible example which will facilitate your learning. Take this comment: 'It's getting kinda late,' and apply it to a given situation; we'll use the following situation: there are two people who are attending a party. One of the individuals, the driver, is having a great time, and even though it is getting late it seems that he would like to stay. The second individual, the passenger, who is reliant on the first individual for a ride home is getting tired and wishes to go home. This wish is constant, although, this individual would feel out of place asking to leave because the other person, the driver seems to be having a great time. So, the second individual approaches the first and says: 'When do you think we'll be leaving?' The first person replies that he has no idea; then, the second person adds: 'It's getting kinda late.' Do you see the unconscious communication?"

"I must say that I don't." Jose replied.

"Well, let's think about it. Think about the wording.

The second person could have just said: 'It's getting late, I'd like to go home.' But he used the words: 'kinda late,' which indicate that 1) he feels some hesitation in approaching the first person, and 2) that it would be ok to stay a little longer."

"But I thought you said that the second individual really wanted to leave. Why then would he imply that it would be ok to stay longer?" Jose asked.

"He didn't mean to. It was his unconscious attitude of feeling bad about asking that dictated what would be said; and not only that, it was an intentional act of the unconscious to get that point across even though the individual in question had no idea what they were really communicating. And the first individual unconsciously caught on to what was being said; so the unconscious drive to stay a little longer kicked in, and, in this example, we'll say that the driver did stay, but only a little longer"

"I see." Jose said.

I went on, "But you don't see everything. There need not be any verbal transfer to make a communication real. Most of our information transfer is done unconsciously by way of body language."

Jose stiffened himself in his chair and said, "What if I don't move? What does that tell you?"

"It tells me a lot!" I replied.

"But I'm not moving, thus I'm not giving you any body language to go on. How can you derive communication from that?"

"Well it all depends on the context of the situation, but you are always communicating something. Take, for instance, this situation; I know what the context is therefore I know that you are refusing to communicate, and that in itself is a communication. I can derive from the context that you are testing out a certain notion that you had, that is, that if you don't move you are not using body language. And, if you were adept in the language of the body you would have known from my smile, that occurred at the exact moment you stiffened up, that I knew exactly what you were doing."

"How would I have known that from your smile?" Jose asked.

"Think about it. You stiffened up and I smiled. You could only extrapolate that through cause and effect that the smile was in response to your body language, and that my smile gave away my amusement at your attempt to confound me."

"OK, I'll give you that." Jose added.

"It's amazing what the unconscious mind can do without our knowledge. Take for instance the following example. A mature female, when being introduced to a potential mate, will examine the male's fingernails, teeth, hair, shoes and anything else that will give away good or bad hygiene. But, if you ask her later if she did those things she will completely deny it, and she'll be telling the truth, as far as she knows. You see, the unconscious mind did it all."

"That's amazing." Jose seemed astonished.

"Anyway, it was also a communication. If the male had noticed what she was doing he could have deduced that she was in the market for a mate, which, potentially, could be very useful information."

"It certainly could. As a matter of fact I'm going to make a mental note to remember that." We both laughed.

I said, "Every moment you are communicating such information, every nuance of your bodies movement, or lack of movement as we've learned, is communicating tons of information about your mood, your thought processes or anything that runs through your mind. But there is also the phenomenon of conversations between two or more people's unconscious minds."

"What do you mean?" Jose asked.

"Well... A request on the part of one individual's unconscious can be replied to with an answer by another person's unconscious mind. Say you're on a date, and you are wondering whether or not the girl you're with wants you to kiss her. First, you might move in a little closer, putting your face closer to hers; now that was an unconscious request made by you; basically asking if it would be ok for you to kiss her. Second, she swells up her shoulders and licks her lips; that was an unconscious reply that the answer is yes."

Jose said, "I think I understand. All that you described took place without them knowing, right. But what now?"

"You would suddenly feel like it would be ok to kiss her. That feeling would be conveyed to you by your unconscious mind."

"I get what you've been telling me so far, but what has it got to do with Adam and Eve?" Jose asked.

I said, "Well, they ate the fruit of knowledge and became acutely aware of what the full implications are of what we've just barely touched upon. They knew that they were exposed completely, that nothing could be hidden from one another; and also, they became aware of all their unconscious communications and what they meant—"

Jose broke in, "And they knew they were naked!"

I added, "That must have been nightmarish for them."

"Why?" Jose asked.

I replied, "I won't answer that, and hopefully you'll never have to find out."

"If you insist."

"I do." I emphatically stated. "But one question for you."

"Ask."

"What do you think is meant in the scripture where it stated that they tried to cover themselves?"

Jose took a moment. He said, "I really don't know."

"Well, my theory is that they immediately tried hiding what they were now aware of communicating out of shame for having their true thoughts known."

"That would make sense."

"Good. Just don't think about this topic too much, ok?"

"I won't," Jose replied sounding somewhat daunted.